BRITISH RAILWAY
SOUTHERN REGION ELECTRICS IN COLOUR

For the Modeller and Historian

Bruce Oliver

Ian Allan
PUBLISHING

Title page:
An up Brighton–Victoria fast service, formed of '6PUL' No 3002, leaves Patcham Tunnel in November 1964.

Above:
Heading for Victoria on 17 April 1984, '4CEP' No 1525 is dwarfed by the spectacular coastal scenery between Abbot's Cliff and Martello Tunnels, near to the site of former Warren Staff Halt.

First published 2008

ISBN 978 0 7110 3258 3

All rights reserved.

© Bruce Oliver 2008

Published by Ian Allan Publishing Ltd, Hersham, Surrey KT12 4RG

Printed in England by Ian Allan Printing Ltd, Hersham, Surrey KT12 4RG.

Code: 0804/B3

Visit the Ian Allan Publishing website at
www.ianallanpublishing.com

All photographs by the author

CONTENTS

INTRODUCTION

When invited to compose a book of colour photographs, in accordance with the cover title, my immediate reaction was one of caution, given the breadth and depth of the subject. There already exists a useful library of books with Southern Electric in the title, including some excellent productions in full colour. Though I seek not to compete with these, the opportunity presented itself to pursue developments since the mid-1960s, with greater emphasis upon the 'middle years' of the late 1960s and 1970s, that found little favour with railway photographers. BR(SR) green had been covered quite thoroughly by photographers but, since that era, it was not until the colourful final years of Mk 1 stock that irresistible photographic opportunities presented themselves, even for those naturally resistant to pointing a camera sincerely at an electric multiple-unit. The 'middle years', characterised by BR corporate all-blue and blue/grey, tended, by contrast, not to stimulate any great level of enthusiasm. It is, perhaps, necessary to point out that, apart from two relevant pictures of units operating under 25kV wires, I have deliberately excluded anything unconnected to 'the system'; thus the Waterloo & City line ('The Drain'), the Isle of Wight line and Merseyrail units exiled from the Southern do not feature.

The 'Jaffa Cake' livery on the South Eastern Division brought welcome relief in the 1980s, an attractive livery that was short-lived, replaced by Network South East's corporate identity of red, white and blue which, in turn, lasted barely a decade. Since the mid-1990s it has, by contrast, been almost impossible to keep abreast of livery variations, such has been the turmoil of change.

Having decided to source material from my own photographic collection, I have reduced an initial selection of more than 700 potential images down to about 200 pictures. Difficulty inevitably arose in deciding what to leave out. Aware how perceived omissions can so easily be greeted with critical alarm, I therefore ask the reader to bear with me in this vexatious undertaking.

It was decided, in the final analysis, to organise the main selection chronologically, following the progression of unit classes, reference to variations and livery changes being dictated by the space available. Few pictures of 1960s green are offered as this has already been well covered elsewhere and I only started taking pictures when green was about to disappear. The most recent years, not least the year of publication, are deliberately well represented, as things have been changing so very rapidly since 1995, embracing withdrawals, new deliveries and livery changes, the latter affecting Classes 73 and 319 most noticeably.

Following a review of unit classes and locomotives, a selection of pictures to highlight buildings and infrastructure shifts the emphasis gently away from rolling stock. I am particularly keen that features other than the trains themselves shall be included in railway photographs – people, stations, signals and boxes, bridges, signage etc. Without such reference points, subjects can too easily lack the necessary impact to stand on their own. However, portraits do have their place in the interests of detail; this cannot be denied. My other concern is the relevance of history – why things happened as they did, and when.

As this has been, for me, something of a personal odyssey, I have concluded the selection with a slightly self-indulgent miscellany, to include nocturnal studies, pairs of units in the same frame, sets of 'time lapse' pictures at the same location and a few others that, I readily concede, fill no category in particular perhaps they self-selected?

I must express my sincere appreciation to Laurie Mack for his kindness in checking the textual accuracy and for making recommendations where necessary.

Bruce Oliver
June 2007

BIBLIOGRAPHY

I am indebted principally to the following reference sources in both checking facts and researching for this book:

1. *History of the Southern Railway*, C.F. Dendy Marshall, revised R.W. Kidner [Ian Allan 1968]
2. *Railways of the Southern Region*, Geoffrey Body [Patrick Stephens 1984]
3. *Southern Electric Multiple Units, 1898-1948 and 1948-1983*, Colin J. Marsden [Ian Allan 1983]
4. *Southern Region Multiple-Unit Trains*, G.D. Beecroft [Southern Electric Group 1979]
5. For the most recent developments, the annual *British Railways Locomotives and Coaching Stock* volumes [published by Platform 5] have provided an invaluable source of relevant information.

OVERVIEW

First impressions tend to stick, I find. As a wartime baby, whose father's life was taken, I became the focus of attention for his extended family in East Anglia. Thus my mother, based in Southsea, found herself having to transport me to and fro between Portsmouth and Norwich, several times a year during the first five years of my life. I was therefore a frequent observer of railway practice, almost from birth.

My earliest recollection is, without doubt, being passed from lap to lap around a dingy compartment, *en route* from Liverpool Street. My attention was drawn, on this occasion, to the carriage ceiling, the object of my fascination being a raised section with glazed sides. Evidently, I was travelling in a clerestory carriage – perhaps one of Great Eastern origin?

A more important memory, just a few years later, is of my being carried on the shoulders of an adult cousin along the platform at Norwich Thorpe, after our arrival there. As we reached the barrier, I was allowed, from this elevated position, to examine the cab of the locomotive that had brought me from London. I clearly recall streamlining, with the bold cab-side number '2859' - a most striking image and one that remains to this day.

From these early years, there arose comparisons. Liverpool Street was for me, as a child, a cauldron of hell – steam, smoke, dirt and a terrifying level of noise, the impression being one of utter confusion. By contrast, Waterloo offered serenity, order and sanity. Here, trains were inexplicably quiet, conspicuously clean and bright green, a combination of attributes most appealing to an impressionable child. What's more, the trains we used had large picture windows, while the ample accommodation provided took the form of 'winged settees' and upholstered armrests of generous size. The woodwork and fittings were of solid, seemingly indestructible, manufacture; everything, right down to the smallest detail, announced quality. And so it was that from this introduction, my earliest acquaintance with '4COR' motor-coaches, I was to be profoundly influenced by Southern Electric, as much as by the units themselves as by any comparison I then made with the Great Eastern Division of the LNER.

THE MAIN LINES

Southern Railway main line electrification was officially opened for public use on 1 January 1933, when '6PUL' (Nos 3001-20), '6CIT' (Nos 3041-43) (originally '6COR') and '4LAV' units (Nos 2921-53) were introduced into service between London and Brighton/West Worthing. For Brighton services alone, three '5BEL' units (Nos 3051-53) were built, adding glamour to the timetable by the inclusion of an all-Pullman car service. Two and a half years later, on 7 July 1935, the Eastbourne scheme was added to the system, when the '6PAN' units (Nos 3021-37) were delivered, together with the first batch of 10 '2BIL' units (Nos 2001-10), to be followed closely by another batch of 38 in sequence

Below:
'2BIL' No 2067 leads a rake of units on a down Alton service through Raynes Park in March 1965. The platforms here are staggered to suit the dive-under and junction for the Epsom line. Note the Southern Railway lamp standards *in situ*, with characteristic hexagonal shades. Originally, shades carried metal banding at the angles between the facets.

(Nos 2011-48). This development brought main line electrification to Lewes, Newhaven, Seaford, Hastings and Ore. Interestingly, the line from Copyhold Junction to Horsted Keynes was also electrified at the same time. [Unit numbers quoted here had replaced those originally allocated after only a few years; express stock had begun life in the '20xx' series, while semi-fast stock initially occupied a block beginning with No 1890.] More about Brighton later.

My own introduction to this new age came via the electrification of the former LSWR main line to Portsmouth. For this scheme, launched officially on 4 July 1937, fully gangwayed '4COR'/'4RES' units (Nos 3101-29/3054-72) were constructed, joined by a further batch of '2BIL' units (Nos 2049-2116), the latter built to serve both Portsmouth and Alton services. A year later, on 3 July 1938, electrification of the former LBSCR lines to Bognor and Portsmouth was inaugurated, for which services '4BUF' units (Nos 3073-85) joined a further delivery of '4COR' stock (Nos 3130-55), along with the final batch of '2BIL' units (Nos 2117-52).

I, as a teenager living in Southsea and one increasingly interested in railways, found myself again making comparisons, not too far removed from those I had made little more than a decade earlier. Electric services from Portsmouth to both the north and the east were, by the 1950s, well established but steam operation to the west and throughout for freight services, remained in evidence right up to its final week on the Southern in July 1967 if, by then, thinned by the infiltration of diesel units and locomotives.

THE OPINIONS OF AN OBSERVER

Though it may have been an inconvenient truth for steam aficionados, from which set I did not exactly dissociate myself, it was, in the 1950s, inescapably apparent that services to the north and east of Portsmouth enjoyed a reputation for reliability, cleanliness, comfort and commendable speed. And, to their credit, these services were years ahead of their time, running, as they did, to a regular interval timetable. It was not lost upon me at the time that the travelling public - as distinct from steam railway enthusiasts - would have voted unhesitatingly for the style of service on offer to the north and to the east, rather than that to the west, where the timetable lacked structure and trains were slow, unpredictable and (in the public's mind) smelly and dirty.

Had the question been put to me at the time – *how would you run a railway, if the offer came your way?* – I am sure my response would have been unequivocal: namely, that services should attract public support for all the very best reasons, implying the principles of sound business practice, as exemplified by that paradigm of success, Southern Electric. This would be tedious, maybe, for die-hard steam enthusiasts – for whom railways were ever perceived as having been designed for no purpose other than their own personal entertainment – but attractive to those with an ear to public opinion.

The history of Southern Electric is already well documented. With this in mind, my task is to attempt a fresh approach – an expression more of hope than expectation, maybe? Nevertheless, I will endeavour to embrace features of the electrified railway that I have come to regard as important as the units themselves. Essentially, it is a personal account, a blend of narrative, factual detail, opinion and observation, without any claim to being a definitive statement.

Photography captures the moment but much is to be found in most photographs, on closer inspection, that pre-dates the intended subject itself. Indeed, trees, buildings, telegraph poles, road vehicles and fashions – quite apart from railway architecture and infrastructure – can define a period quite precisely. Trees can be seen to have grown remarkably – or even to have disappeared – in the interval between the taking of photographs, several years apart at the same location. Meanwhile, new buildings spring up, while others may have been either demolished or altered almost beyond recognition. It is true that, since the age of steam, encroachment of lineside vegetation and the positioning of high security fencing represent a major change, denying photographic opportunities where once views were unobstructed.

Station buildings provide a most significant association with the past, often having stood the test of time, while all about them has responded to the inexorable march of progress. Sadly, there was an infamous determination to demolish 'the past' during the 1960s, though, it should be remarked, a not dissimilar rejection of the old order had been very much in play during the 1920s and 1930s, when rebuilding of stations was deemed feasible, fashionable and necessary. In some cases, rebuilding was an inevitable consequence of track widening and the expansion of facilities. The Southern Railway undertook a major rebuilding programme throughout its territory in the inter-war period, evidence of which sets the scene for much present-day photography. Liveries have changed, signalboxes have disappeared, track layouts have been rationalised and two generations of electric trains have come and gone, but buildings survive, offering an important lifeline of continuity. At many locations, such as Ramsgate, Havant and Exeter Central, the Southern Railway stamped its imprimatur of ownership emphatically upon the system it had inherited.

The period style between the wars, classified 'Art Deco', is characterised by geometric figuration, clean lines and an inescapable spirit of self-confidence. Buildings were designed to be functional and efficient and most still are, with little alteration having been required over subsequent decades. The Southern Railway's grasp of 'purpose building' was certainly both thorough and imaginative. The Southern Railway was, in every sense of the word, modern, its ultimate statement of the genre being the iconic station structures erected on the Chessington South branch, opened throughout for public use on 28 May 1939. Southern Railway signalboxes, imposing examples of which are still to be seen all over the system, echo the mood of the age – with their sweeping lines, angle-faceted ends and flat, hooded roofs. 'Alternative use', a term perhaps tinged with cynical veneration, may now apply to many of these grand statements of the age but their survival is a reminder of the days when Southern Electric was synonymous with progress.

WORLD WAR 2 AND NATIONALISATION

World War 2 might have brought progress to an abrupt standstill, as the Southern entered a period of air attack, being itself very much in the front line. However, at the start of the war, the Southern launched its first purpose-built suburban electric multiple-unit design of the Bulleid period, bearing outward resemblance to the first 76 '2HAL' units (Nos 2601-76), then recently supplied for the 1939 Gillingham and Maidstone schemes. A supplementary batch of '2HAL' stock (Nos 2677-92) was delivered in 1940. Despite the need for centres of engineering to support the war effort, the Southern was certainly still

Above:
'2HAL' No 2634 leads a six-car train from Buriton Tunnel in August 1969, on a stopping service from Waterloo to Portsmouth & Southsea. It is green, with small yellow patch, the '2V' identifying the guard's-van vehicle.

moving forward with new ideas germinating, not least of which was the Southern's extraordinary new Pacific steam locomotive design, contrasting curiously with the direction investment had taken during the previous decade.

When nationalisation occurred in 1948, the railways were still responding to the consequences of wartime depredation. Levels of investment, maintenance and refurbishment might, understandably, be expected to have declined in comparison with the standard the Southern Railway set itself during the 1930s. However, Mr Bulleid's brief, if idiosyncratic, reign as Chief Mechanical Engineer endowed the Southern with a miscellany of carriages, extensive in number and handsome in appearance, celebrated for their comfort, elegance, spaciousness and quality – quite apart from his audacious fleet of Pacifics. While these splendid main line carriages were (almost) exclusively for steam haulage, the later

builds of post-war electric stock achieved no less a standard for suburban services, being, in their class, outstanding.

SUBURBAN EVOLUTION

The image of British Railways was brought to bear upon the four former railway companies with remarkable speed. Not only did Robert Riddles, who is alleged wisely to have favoured railway electrification, design the new Standard locomotive classes, resulting in the building of 999 steam locomotives, but Standard MkI passenger coaching stock emerged from the various carriage works inevitably to dispatch, by cascade process, thousands of veterans to the scrap-yard. The Southern's stock of older vehicles, including electric multiple-units, was not exempt from the consequences of modernisation during the 1950s.

Suburban electric units had been created, in typical Southern good-housekeeping tradition, by converting, for further use, steam stock of pre-grouping origin, and from all three of the constituent companies (the London & South Western, London Brighton & South Coast and the South Eastern & Chatham Railways). Exceptions to this practice were brand new units for the

Guildford 'New Line' and South Eastern suburban electrification schemes of 1925, successors to the trail-blazing LSWR units for the East Putney and Wimbledon launch of 25 October 1915. Even older than these LSWR units were the eight '2SL' units (latterly Nos 1801-08) and four '2WIM' sets (Nos 1809-12), converted in 1929/30 from overhead wire motors and trailers respectively, built in 1908/09. The '2SLs' and '2WIMs' were for use on the inner suburban South London and Wimbledon-West Croydon lines and were numbered 1901-12 when first converted for third-rail operation.

Outer suburban three-car units were augmented during the 1940s by the insertion of a second trailer, becoming '4SUB' units. The new trailers were of Bulleid design, causing the sets to lose their uniform profile. Two-car trailer sets had, prior to their disbandment, been used to augment three-car units as external attachments. Suburban stock pre-dating the Bulleid era lasted into the early 1960s, when displaced by the final batch of BR Standard 'EPB' stock.

Between 1934 and 1936, the small fleet of a dozen two-car suburban units (the '2SL' and '2WIM' sets) was augmented by 78 units converted from standard LSWR steam-hauled coaches, designated '2NOL'. These units underwent alterations over the years but, by 1948, were finally divided into two distinct batches: Nos 1813-50, operating with first-class accommodation, in partnership with '2BIL' and '2HAL' stock and Nos 1851-90, which were third-class only and were specifically diagrammed for Waterloo-Windsor services.

Bulleid '4SUB' units came in seven batches: Nos 4101-10, 4111-20, 4121-30, 4355-77, 4277-99, 4621-66 and 4667-754, the last three incorporating three open saloons and a compartment trailer. While Bulleid '4SUB' construction was in full swing, two experimental double-deck units were released to traffic from 1949. Production went no further but the two '4DD' units (Nos 4001/02, later 4901/02) operated between London and Dartford until their withdrawal on 1 October 1971.

Prior to the change in direction that established the EPB era, there were a few first generation additions to stock, bringing two 'HAL'-style '4LAV' units (Nos 2954-55) and seven Bulleid-profile '2HAL' units (Nos 2693-99) into service. Finally, '2HAL' No 2700 appeared in 1955, at a time when accident damage had predicated the early retirement of a few pre-World War 2 units.

THE SECOND GENERATION

Upon completion of the Bulleid '4SUB' order of suburban units in 1951, delivery of '4EPB' (Electro Pneumatic Brake) stock commenced, a design operationally incompatible with all that had gone before. Recognised by their 'Bulleid' profile, these units carried forward Southern Railway influence almost to the end of the 20th century. Delivered between 1951 and 1957, they came in three batches (Nos 5001-15, 5016-53 and 5101-5260), though four extra units were created from spare vehicles from 1960. Interestingly, the Southern's penchant for recycling material was revisited in 1959, when the frames of withdrawn '2NOL' units were used in the construction of a batch of 34 '2EPB' units (Nos 5651-84). These retained the Bulleid profile, a style that had already been superseded with delivery of two batches of British Railways Mk I '2EPB' units (Nos 5701-11/12-78) between 1953 and 1958; No 5779 was an addition. As the abandonment of electrification on the suburban circuit in Newcastle upon Tyne approached, an additional 15 Eastleigh-built units became available,

Below:
The second batch of '4SUB' stock was delivered in 1946 and with these units, the SR dispensed with the sloping outer end roof, fitted to the first 10 units. In June 1969 Surbiton's Southern Railway signalbox stands proudly as No 4112, from the second batch, passes.

returning to their place of birth, to be refurbished in 1963 (as Nos 5781-95) for further use on the Southern. 1960-63 saw the final order of 70 BR Standard '4EPB' units arrive in two batches, 5301-56 (Phase I) and 5357-70 (Phase II).

Frames from withdrawn '2NOL' units also found re-employment in the construction of a series of '2HAP' units (Nos 5601-36), which were geared to express train standards. These units, though constructed as late as 1958, carried Bulleid-profile bodywork, yet were contemporary with Standard profile examples of the same class, then under construction for use in Kent. They operated on the South Eastern but a large batch was transferred to the South Western Division in 1969, when declassification of first-class accommodation took place, this sub-class being redefined as '2SAP'. Within the space of barely a year, these units were transferred yet again, this time to the Central Division, with their first-class accommodation restored for use on 'Coastway' services. About six years later, they all moved back to the London area, where suburban use in the Central Division required declassification of first-class accommodation for the second time. In their final years, selected vehicles from these units found further use in re-formed '4EPB' units. From 1982, EPB suburban stock underwent a programme of refurbishment, when renumbering matched unit numbers with the last four figures of their TOPS six-character identities. Face-lifted Bulleid-profile '4EPBs' (Class 415/4) filled the 54xx series, while others followed the

pattern: 53xx (Class 415/6) units became 56xx, 57xx (Class 416/2) became 62xx and 56xx (Class 416/3) became 63xx.

THE SOUTH EASTERN DIVISION MAIN LINES

Delivery of Southern Railway express multiple-unit stock, reformations apart, had ended with the '4BUF' and '4COR' requirements for the 1938 Bognor/Portsmouth scheme. It was not until 1956 that the first Standard EPB-compatible express units appeared, comprising four '4CEP' (Nos 7101-04) and two '4BEP' (Nos 7001-02) units. These were to be found, at the time, on Bognor/Portsmouth diagrams amongst other duties, prior to the design being constructed in vast numbers for the main line electrification schemes in Kent. However, '4CEP' units, via reallocation, continued to be seen on Central Division duties over the years. Interestingly, the very last deliveries of '4CEP' units, Nos 7205-11, found use, as new, on 'rush hour' duties between Waterloo and Portsmouth; this was but a brief interlude prior to their transfer to Kent. It is perhaps worthy of mention that internal hard surfaces for the Kent deliveries were of a plastic material, whereas the six pre-production units had followed established BR Mk 1 hauled stock tradition in the use of various woods, which were identified by small plates.

Main lines in Kent were electrified in two stages, in 1959 and 1961/62. Broadly speaking, the former London Chatham & Dover Railway main lines were first to be converted, those of South Eastern

Railway origin following two years later. Many new units built for these schemes had spent time stored on the 'down' line between Horsted Keynes and Ardingly, also in sidings at Gatwick, Lancing and Ford. Some did see interim use on Central Division services. '4CEP' mass-production embraced three batches, Nos 7105-53 (Phase I), 7154-7204 (Phase II) and, finally, Nos 7205-11, while '4BEP' units came in two batches, Nos 7003-12 (Phase I) and Nos 7013-7022 (Phase II). Phase II express units received Commonwealth bogies, in response to dissatisfaction with the riding characteristics of the Phase I order. Phase I and Phase II units, upon refurbishment, became (under TOPS) Nos 1506-62 and 1563-1621, respectively, while Nos 1501-05 took vehicles from Nos 7001/02 and 7101-04. Briefly, from 1983, a few '4CEP' units had spare buffet cars substituted for trailers, becoming '4TEP' (27xx).

In 1975, '4CEP' No 7153 was rebuilt at Eastleigh, with a view to refurbishing the entire class. Guard's vans adjacent to

From 1978, a programme of refurbishment for the entire series was undertaken at Swindon, a visible consequence being renumbering and the installation of hopper ventilators, replacing those of Standard sliding design. Interestingly, a few former locomotive-hauled vehicles were adapted for use in the programme. The programme ensured that buffet-car units were never again to be seen operating in Kent. Initially, TOPS six-character set numbers were carried (411506 etc) but this was soon abandoned, with a return to the traditional Southern four-digit reference (1506 etc). The prototype unit, No 7153, was eventually renumbered No 1500; its sliding ventilators were never exchanged for hoppers, which was, given the experience of 'hopper draughts', a most fortunate decision.

Within the programme of refurbishment, Portsmouth services received refurbished '4BEP' units (No 2301-07), to replace the '4BIG' units, then reallocated to the Central Division.

between batches become evident when units are examined more closely, roof-clutter being a feature of earlier deliveries.

In 1973, Standard profile '2HAP' units also underwent re-formation, when first-class accommodation was declassified in units Nos 6001-21 and 6024-44, the units redefined as '2SAP' and renumbered 5901-42. In this guise, they operated Windsor line services. [Nos 6022/23 had already been set aside for experimentation with Tightlock couplings.] However, from 1979, declassified accommodation was reinstated and the '2SAP' description deleted. Reallocated from Ramsgate in 1982, a squadron of former '2HAP' units joined the Central Division on 'Coastway' services. Already coupled in semi-permanent pairs and redefined as '4CAP', the two batches (Nos 3201-13, 3301-11) distinguished between '1951' and '1957' control equipment.

CENTRAL DIVISION DEVELOPMENTS

Brighton was the setting for poignant obsequies when, in 1964, examples of the first main line stock ever to enter service – the '6PUL', '6PAN', '6CIT' and '4LAV' units dating from 1931-35 – were displaced from services, with the arrival on the scene of Phase I Class 4CIG/BIG units (Nos 7301-36/7031-48). The new units soon had the full service in their grasp, one that eventually embraced all points between Ore and Portsmouth Harbour. It must be pointed out the original Brighton main line units, as listed above, never normally undertook duties over lines to Bognor and Portsmouth, where '4COR'/'BUF' stock operated from the outset in 1938. When the original Brighton main line stock was finally withdrawn from regular service on 'home territory', 10 units, re-formed as Nos 3041-50 without refreshment cars, enjoyed a brief stay of execution, incredibly to be found operating peak services between Victoria and Ramsgate.

At about the same time, other first-generation Southern Electric units were re-formed. Five '4RES' units (Nos 3054/55/57/59/61) had their restaurant cars replaced by Pullman cars, vehicles released upon withdrawal of the '6PUL' units; No 3061 was renumbered 3056. Other '4RES' units (Nos 3062/64/66/67/69-71) were reclassified '4COR(N)', equipped with redundant trailers from 'PUL' and 'PAN' stock, Nos 3062/64 becoming 3065/68. Meanwhile, three

Above:
On 1 April 1967 '4CEPs' Nos 7174 and 7122 formed the very first revenue-earning electric service to arrive at Southampton. They had travelled from Folkestone Harbour, bringing a large party of Italian seamen to the port to crew a liner. The train had travelled via Factory Junction at Stewarts Lane.

driving cabs were converted to form open passenger accommodation, with a single guard's van area replacing two second-class compartments in the trailer composite. A public address system was installed, along with new gangway connections, Mk 2e seating and double-glazing, though Standard sliding ventilators were retained. Control equipment was updated in line with developments.

In their final years of service on the South Eastern, 18 '4CEP' units were reduced to '3CEP' status (renumbered 1101-18), by the removal of a trailer vehicle. This effectively enhanced their power/weight ratio, perhaps permitting competition on more level terms with their Class 375 replacements.

For semi-fast and stopping services, 173 '2HAP' units (Nos 6001-173) were constructed between 1957 and 1963, the first 42 members of the class displacing '2HAL' stock on the Gillingham and Maidstone schemes. Subsequent batches were built for Kent Phase I electrification in 1959 (Nos 6043-105), Kent Phase II in 1961 (Nos 6106-146) and the South Western Division (Nos 6147-73) in 1963. Detail differences

restaurant cars had been rebuilt as '(griddle' cars, the units (Nos 3056/65/68) reclassified '4GRI' (renumbered 3086-88), for use on Waterloo-Portsmouth services, which they subsequently shared with the '4BUF' units, recently displaced by the invasion of second generation '4CIG'/'BIG' units on Victoria services. '4RES' No 3072's kitchen car had been converted into a buffet car in 1955, following fire damage.

Following the Bournemouth electrification, it was the arrival, on the Central Division, of '4VEP' units in great numbers – and Phase II '4CIG' deliveries – that saw the elimination of all first generation stock, to include the three '5BEL' units. Unsympathetically, these elegant units were required to end their lives reliveried in British Rail blue and grey. The Brighton Belle ran for the last time on 30 April 1972.

Briefly in 1964/65, two '4COR' units (Nos 3124/48) were restyled as a semi-permanent eight-car formation, for use on the South Western Division, where the outer motor driving vehicles were, most strikingly, '6PUL' in origin.

Finally, and most unusually, two units were adapted for diesel haulage, traction equipment having been removed from the '2BIL' and '4COR' units chosen for the purpose. It was 1963 when the ex-2BIL vehicles became the outer members of a seven-car formation, the five internal members having previously served as '4SUB' trailers. Set 900's extraordinary 'non-push-pull' assembly of carriages operated between London and Tunbridge Wells, via Oxted, of

necessity always towed by a diesel locomotive. And then, in 1965, two ex-'4COR' motor vehicles, with traction equipment removed, were adapted for 'push-pull' operation by Class 33/1 diesel locomotives, the four internal vehicles of this six-car formation being redundant 'PUL' and 'PAN' trailers. Set 601 saw service on the Oxted line and, subsequently, between Clapham Junction and Kensington Olympia. It served as a test bed for the introduction of push-pull operation on Bournemouth services from 1967.

LIVERIES

Southern Region electric units had continued the tradition of green paint – of various hues – throughout the first 18 years of nationalisation, until the imposition of British Rail Blue in the mid-1960s. Surprisingly quickly, even units of Southern Railway origin emerged in the new, comparatively drab, blue uniform. About the same time, it was decided also to place yellow warning panels on locomotives and multiple-unit stock. The process came through several stages: green, green with a yellow rectangle, blue with a yellow rectangle, surviving green with full yellow end and, finally, blue with full yellow end. In respect of the various hues of green, early BR green was a light shade, one that might have suggested premature fading.

In the later 1950s, the better remembered varnished darker green became standard issue. This survived

Above:
'4BUF' No 3082 leads a down Portsmouth fast past the staggered down platform at Raynes Park in March 1965. It was unusual, here, to catch a buffet unit not sandwiched between two 'COR' units.

conditions better than its paler predecessor though, towards the end of the green era, the dubious economy of an unvarnished finish was introduced. This, frankly, was a disaster, as it attracted dirt. Units, as a consequence, looked dreary – as bad, if not worse, than those that had been transformed by the application of a gloomy shade of blue. An imaginative move – and such relief in the late 1960s – was the decision to extend the blue/grey corporate image, then currently in use on locomotive-hauled stock, to non-suburban multiple-units. Thus, all Southern second generation main line units became transformed in appearance, and relatively quickly. However, surviving first generation stock, such as '4COR' units, received no such preferment. The Bournemouth deliveries of 1967 lasted only briefly in their original all-blue livery, as did the recently built '4VEP' stock. Experimentally, perhaps, '4VEP' No 7808 was granted the blue/grey treatment some time in advance of others in its class. Over a decade later, EPB suburban units – those face-lifted in the 1980s – emerged in blue/grey, and this brightened the suburban image. A leap of greater imagination was taken in the early 1980s, when '4CEP' units in Kent began to appear in a three-tone livery of buff and brown, divided by a band or orange. Nicknamed 'Jaffa Cake', it was truly a most remarkable departure from convention, greatly admired and welcomed. Unfortunately, the timing was a little late, events being overtaken by the formation of Network South East, when re-branding of BR's London & South East Sector established a new, distinct image of its own. NSE's initial choice of banding in red, white and blue had appeared awkward at cab-ends, where the bands turned through a sharp angle to reach roof level. This was later modified, with a gentler, curved effect at the transition point. The original shade of blue did not wear well, being vulnerable to both the elements and washing plant treatment. The replacement darker blue certainly lasted much better and was not unpleasing.

With privatisation came a cascade of different liveries, presenting the photographer with a startling menu of variety. Indeed, since 1995, keeping up with the frequency of change has been quite demanding. The Connex livery, mainly white, sprinkled with yellow, was

an unfortunate choice, being entirely inappropriate in respect of wear and tear. South West Trains, a franchise awarded to the bus operator, Stagecoach, settled, unsurprisingly, for a combination of colours resembling the parent group's bus livery. Following roughly the lines adopted by NSE, the effect was not inartistic, markedly in contrast with the treatment of Stagecoach's bus fleets at the time. More recently, the company modified its image quite strikingly, while retaining the essential elements of the original idea. South Eastern Trains, following a trend set by the original Connex image, chose a basically white livery, relieved by touches of colour and company logos. Prior to the collapse of Connex South Eastern, its modern units had begun to appear in a revised livery, one incorporating a measure of blue. Govia Southern, meanwhile, went for tradition in its choice of colours, if not exactly in style and balance. Two-tone green and white provided a most welcome change but a preponderance of white dominated the finished product.

ELECTRIFICATION EXPANSION AND CONTRACTION

The Bournemouth scheme of 1967, the first major development since the completion of the Kent electrification in 1961, saw the introduction of push-pull working, multiple-unit style, with '4REP' tractor units providing the motive power, while '3TC' and '4TC' trailer units augmented formations.

These trailer units, created by a marriage of new and former locomotive-hauled vehicles, were push-pull operated by Class 33/1 diesel locomotives, specially adapted for the purpose, for the journey between Bournemouth and Weymouth.

Initially, twelve '4REP' units had been constructed for the scheme but numbers were subsequently increased to fifteen, while the '3TC' units were enlarged to become '4TC'. When the new order took over in July 1967, stopping services were entrusted to the first twenty members of the '4VEP' series, in which second/standard class accommodation featured 3+2 seating in open saloons, with doors to individual bays. Within the space of about six years, this class of unit had swelled to 194 in number, for use on all three divisions, though one such unit (No 7739), disbanded at an early stage for experimental reasons, never recovered its original identity. The '8VAB' unit, No 8001, including a buffet car, had been devised to operate alongside '4REP'/'TC' diagrams.

Curiously, the very first revenue-earning service on the newly electrified line to Southampton was undertaken by a pair of '4CEP' units (Nos 7122 and 7174), bringing a party of Italian seamen from Folkestone (via Factory Junction) to Southampton, to crew a ship in the docks. The date was 1 April 1967, with over three months of steam operation on the South Western Division still to run.

Electrification between Tonbridge and Bopeep Junction was opened to public use on 27 April 1986, while two further schemes to be authorised were opened by Network South East in 1987 (from Sanderstead to East Grinstead) and in 1990 (between Portcreek/Farlington Junctions and Eastleigh/St. Denys). The latter scheme saw the introduction of through electric services between Waterloo and Portsmouth via Eastleigh and Fareham, also between Southampton and Portsmouth. Electrification enabled the subsequent introduction of through services between Brighton and Basingstoke/Waterloo, also Victoria via Haywards Heath to Bournemouth, later cut back to Southampton.

Eurostar services commenced on 14 November 1994, for which development came the reconstruction at Waterloo (Platforms 20-24) and the building of the Linford Street Junction curve (connecting the LSWR and LCDR main lines). Also, a reception area at Dollands Moor had been constructed for Eurotunnel Shuttle

Below:
Portcreek Junction in July 1966, prior to the building of the road bridge. A 12-coach rake of 'COR'/'BUF'/'COR' stock crosses the water *en route* to Portsmouth Harbour, on a fast service, with unit No 3138 taking the lead. The units are seen here in full BR(SR) green livery, with small yellow warning panel in place.

Left:
No E6006 was from the original batch of
electro-diesels, subsequently designated
Class 73. It is approaching St John's cutting,
Woking, with a short-lived '3TC' unit next to
the locomotive. The few '3TCs' were, not
long afterwards, expanded to '4TC'.

services and freight. On 28 September
2003, the 25kV Channel Tunnel Rail
Link dedicated route from Dollands
Moor to Fawkham Junction was opened,
bringing electrification to a section of
the former Gravesend West branch.

Since the mid-1990s, Eurostar has
brought exotic Class 373 units to former
Southern Railway territory, where,
initially, they shared track with
obsolescent second generation units.
However, the opening of the final stage
from Southfleet Junction. to Stratford and
St. Pancras has led to Eurostar services
abandoning the route westwards into
Waterloo. Usefully, the link to St Pancras
is to be shared with new high-speed local
services from east Kent to London
operated by Class 395 units.

Third-rail closures to have taken
place are, in summary: Crystal Palace
High Level branch from Nunhead
(20 September 1954); Copyhold Junction
to Horsted Keynes (28 October 1963);
Coulsdon North terminus (4 September
1983); Holborn Viaduct terminus
(26 January 1990); Dover Marine
(24 September 1994); Elmers End
to Addiscombe (terminus) and
Sanderstead, also Wimbledon to
West Croydon (31 May 1997). A further
third-rail loss was the Sturt Lane curve
from Frimley (21 July 1966).

FURTHER SECOND GENERATION
DEVELOPMENTS

When steam finally disappeared from
the Southern in July 1967, Waterloo
became host to the new '4REP' and
'4VEP' units, operating alongside the
30-year-old '2BIL', '2HAL' and '4COR'
(plus '4BUF'/'GRI') units. Parallel
operation continued with pre-World
War 2 stock on Portsmouth services
until 1970, after which the '4COR' units
lasted for a further year on Alton/

Reading line diagrams, following the
demise of the '2BIL' and '2HAL' classes.
'4COR' stock succumbed finally to
withdrawal in 1972, following a swansong
on 'Coastway' services operating east
and west from Brighton. With '2BIL' and
'2HAL' units already consigned to
history, displaced by '4COR' stock a year
or two earlier on services for which the
two-car units had originally been built,
the first generation of Southern Railway
main-line units took its final bow.

Portsmouth services from Waterloo
were brought up to date with the first
deliveries of Phase II '4CIG'/'BIG' units
(Nos 7337-57/7049-58). These units
featured a more Spartan ambience than
that of their well-appointed Phase I
predecessors. Stopping services had
already been infiltrated and taken over
by further deliveries of '4VEP' units; in
the event, the changeover was completed
swiftly, new units having flooded the
system to oust surviving examples of
'2BIL' and '2HAL'. Deliveries of Phase II
'4CIG' stock eventually took the series to
No 7438, with allocations split between
Central and South Western Divisions.

Electrification was extended from
Bournemouth to Weymouth in 1988.
In connection with this, 24 new five-car

units, Class 442 (Nos 2401-24), were built
for the service from Waterloo – but the
traction equipment was secondhand,
passed down from withdrawn Class
4REP units in a process executed in
stages. This programme resulted in many
extraordinary temporary formations,
with necessary renumbering of units.
During the following decade, Class 442
use was extended to certain Portsmouth
line services, requiring wider use of
'4CIG' units on the Bournemouth route.
This practice had ceased altogether by
2004, when Class 444 'Desiro' units
arrived to replace second-generation
units on Waterloo-Portsmouth services.

Reference must here be made to
'4CEP' units, inasmuch many units,
displaced by the arrival of third
generation units in Kent, latterly found
further use by South West Trains on
services to both Portsmouth and
Bournemouth/Weymouth. They also
reached Brighton on services from
Basingstoke. Not long before their
withdrawal, the seven 'greyhound'
'4BEP' units (Nos 2301-07) swapped
buffet cars with trailers from existing
'4CEP' units but retained their numbers
in the 23xx series (becoming Nos 2311-
17), in order that 'greyhound' status
should not be conferred on under-used

Below:
The inaugural special run from Waterloo to
Weymouth, a major publicity event launching
the electrification to the Dorset terminus
took place on 14 April 1988. Class 442 units
Nos 2401 and 2403 are seen coming round
the curve at Pirbright.

vehicles. The donating '4CEP' units were renumbered 2321-27, which was, at least, logical, even though the buffets were out of use. In their final form, '4CEP' units Nos 1697-99 were mounted on a combination of Mk 4, Mk 6 and B5 bogies. By displacement, '4CEP' trailers were to be found as buffet-car replacements in the additional 'greyhound' units Nos 1392-99 (former 4BIG units), all except one having come from '4CEP' units reduced to '3CEP' form (Nos 1101-18). Two 'CEP'/'BEP' units, also in three-car form, operated the Lymington shuttle until their demise.

RENUMBERING IN THE COMPUTER AGE

Prior to their replacement, '4REP' units had been redefined in the '20xx' series, within a TOPS renumbering scheme that had affected all second-generation multiple-units. Upon renumbering, the '4VEP' units first reappeared in the 30xx and 31xx series, until later refreshed, when numbers in the 34xx and 35xx series became their final identities. '4CEP' units had already been renumbered upon refurbishment. When it came to the turn of '4CIG' units, they occupied the 11xx and 12xx series before finally settling down in the 17xx (Phase I),

Below:
'3COP' No 1409 passes the signalbox on the approach to Lewes with an Eastbourne–Brighton service on 18 June 2001. This 'CIG'/'BIG' sub-class had the first-class sections gutted, the space opened out for standard use.

19xx (Phase I, Mk6 motor bogies) and 18xx (Phase II) series, when 'face-lifted'. Buffet-car units, as long as they survived, were renumbered 21xx (Phase I) and 22xx (Phase II), though hybridisation occurred. For example, some displaced Phase I buffet cars were installed in Phase II '4CIG' units. It was indeed a complicated 'phase'.

'Face-lifting' occupied the late 1980s and early 1990s, when '4CIG' and '4BIG' units were renumbered under TOPS classification. Inevitably, there were various intermediate, short-lived situations, too numerous here to describe in depth. Suffice to say, alterations embraced asbestos removal from Phase I stock, rebuilding of many buffet cars as open stock, initial painting of face-lifted Phase I units in 'Jaffa Cake' livery and the transfer of several '4CIG' units to Ramsgate. Twenty-two 18xx series '4CIG' were further altered, to emerge as the 13xx 'greyhound' sub-class, modified for enhanced performance. They were joined by the similarly enhanced '4BEP' units (23xx) for operation on Portsmouth (and Bournemouth) services. In 1997/98, 11 Class 4CIG/BIG units were partially gutted and rebuilt as three-car, standard class-only '3COP' units (Nos 1401-11), for Connex 'Coastway' services. Some units regained four-car status but retained the 14xx identity.

THE THIRD GENERATION

The prototype ('PEP') experimental third generation units, Nos 4001/02 (four-car) and 2001 (2-car), appeared in

1971/72. These were the basis for Class 508, a squadron of 43 four-car units, delivered in 1979/80. However, these units lasted only briefly on the South Western Division of the Southern, before being transferred, as three-car units, to Merseyside from 1984, when superseded on the South Western Division by Class 455. Remarkably, twelve face-lifted Class 508 units (as Nos 508201-212) returned to the Southern in 1998/99 for use on the South Eastern, operating Medway Valley services, amongst other duties. Another three returned south – face-lifted in 2002/03 (as Nos 508301-303) – uniquely for service with Silverlink between Euston and Watford Junction.

Arriving in three distinct batches, the first Class 455 order (Nos 5801-74) was followed immediately by the second (Nos 5701-43), where the number of units equalled that of Class 508. Each member of the latter class was therefore able to donate a trailer vehicle to the replacement Class 455 order. Thus, members of this 'economical' second batch can be identified easily, not only by their smoother front-end design but by the abrupt interruption to profile, resulting from a marriage of styles. The final batch of 20 units (Nos 5901-20) is distinguishable from the second batch by its uniform profile and from the first by the improved front-end design. These deliveries removed from the scene first- and second-generation Southern Electric suburban units on both the South Western and Central Divisions, displacing initially '4SUB' and finally EPB units. All Class 455 units saw service on the South Western division at the time of delivery but the first 46 (Nos 5801-46) eventually found permanent employment on the Central Division, there to displace the last examples of second generation suburban units. These Class 455 transfers had subsequently been joined in 1990/91 by new two-car Class 456 units (Nos 456001-024), a design similar in profile to the 25kV three/four-car Classes 320-322.

Alsthom Class 458 units (Nos 458001-030) were introduced from 2000 on services using the Windsor line platforms at Clapham Junction. Unfortunately, they appeared to be a most unsatisfactory investment, and for a number of reasons. Water ingress, inability to make practical use of gangway connections between units and an inadequate internal communications system numbered amongst other problems, computer associated, that caused the class to be threatened with

withdrawal from service. Most units were mothballed for long periods, though there was never a period when none could be seen in operation. Modifications were made that ameliorated the scant regard in which they had been held. As a consequence, there followed a gradual return to service. Two units, Nos 8001/02, were transferred temporarily to Gatwick Express, as capital reserve, being from the same manufacturer as the Class 460 units, seen in daily service (q.v.).

STRUCTURAL CHANGES

Network South East had been created on 10 June 1986 as an autonomous sector of British Rail. The rolling stock progeny of the NSE Sector was the 'Networker', bringing a design of unit to the entire region that found use in various guises. It was 'Networkers' that saw the elimination of second generation suburban units on the South Eastern Division, with the delivery of Classes 465 (four-car) and 466 (two-car) between 1992 and 1994. The 190 'Networkers' were delivered in four batches, Nos 465001-050 (built by British Rail Engineering Limited), 465151-197 (BREL), 465201-250 (Metro-Cammell) and 466001-043 (GEC Alsthom). After just over a decade in service and well into the era of privatisation, 34 former Metro-Cammell-built units were refurbished, to include a first-class section. They were renumbered from the 4652xx to the 4659xx series for use on main line services, in a supporting role to the Bombardier 'Electrostar' series of units (three-car Nos 375301-310 and four-car Nos 375601-630, 701-715, 801-830 and 901-927), the latter squadron having dispatched the final second generation '4CEP' and '4VEP' units to the graveyard by 2005. [3759xx units featured high-density seating.]

From 1994/95, coastal services in Kent had been served by a batch of 16 express 'Networker' Class 365 units (Nos 365501-516). However, in 2004/05, it was delivery of thirty-six five-car, high-density suburban units (Class 376) that released the Class 4652xx units (referred to above) for refurbishment. This, in turn, allowed the Class 365 units to be modified for use with the other 25kV class members, on services out of King's Cross.

Privatisation of railways took effect over the period 1995-97. Stagecoach became the operator in the former South Western Division, while Connex took control in both the former South Eastern

Above:
No 465234, one of the Metro-Cammell batch of 'Networkers', passes Bickley Junction on a service from the Swanley direction on 11 September 1999. The lines to the right form the Tonbridge Loop to Petts Wood.

and Central Divisions, though these were operated as separate companies. In time, financial/operational problems affected both Connex companies, with an announcement, coming in October 2000, that the South Central company had lost its franchise. Three years later in 2003, the South Eastern company, evidently in even greater difficulties at the time, had its franchise terminated by the Strategic Rail Authority, with the running of the railway placed temporarily in government hands. Meanwhile, the Govia group had been awarded the South Central franchise, reviving the evocative title 'Southern' as its logo. Following a brief period in administration, the South East franchise was also awarded to the Govia group, under the title South Eastern, the two Govia operations retaining their separate identities.

Replacement of second generation express stock over South Eastern lines had begun in earnest with the delivery of the first Bombardier 'Electrostar' units in 1999/2000, yet modernisation on the other two divisions did not effectively take off until 2002, when deliveries of 'Electrostar' Class 377 units (to Govia Southern) and Siemens 'Desiro' Class 450 units (to South West Trains) began. Initially, the South West Trains five-car 'Desiro' Class 444 units (444001-045) replaced second-generation units on Portsmouth services but their use widened, as more units became available. Meanwhile Class 450 deliveries continued, to complete the initial order

(450001-110), followed in 2006 by a further order, taking the series to No 450127. Deliveries of Bombardier Class 377 'Electrostars' to Southern had been completed earlier, the final allocation comprising units Nos 377101-164, 201-215 (dual voltage, for use on 25kV services to Watford), 301-328 (three-car units) and 401-475.

Elimination of second-generation express stock was achieved during 2005 by withdrawal from service of the last examples of '4VEP', '4CEP' and '4CIG' stock – by South West Trains on 26 May (Nos 1396, 3536 and 1398 on the 1135 Waterloo-Bournemouth), South East Trains on 7 October (Nos 3565, 3545 and 3568 on the 1804 Cannon Street-Ashford) and, finally, Southern on 26 November (Nos 3490, 3505 and 3535 on the 1109 Victoria-Brighton). But elimination would not be complete, as SWT had achieved dispensation to employ two '3CIG' units (Nos 1497/98 being former '4CIG' units with a trailer removed) on the Brockenhurst to Lymington Pier shuttles. Sadly, SWT's extravagant 2006 franchise renewal was a public relations fiasco. Popular, iconic Class 442 was withdrawn from service, a move of breathtaking ineptitude, while

converted for use as Class 488 (two-car units Nos 8201-10 and three-car units Nos 8301-19) to operate sandwiched between Class 73 locomotives and Class 489 driving motor luggage vans (Nos 9101-10, formerly boat train driving motor vans 68500-09).

This arrangement lasted until the delivery, in 1999-2000, of eight Alsthom Class 460 units (Nos 460001-008), for use exclusively on Gatwick Express duties. The introduction of these eight-car units had not been uneventfully smooth and, as a consequence, Class 73 operation continued, intermittently, for a further four years.

PARALLEL OPERATIONS 2
THAMESLINK

Class 319 units were introduced in stages (ultimately carrying numbers 319001-013, 214-220, 361-386 and 421-460), between 1987 and 1990, in connection with the reincarnation of cross-London services, via Farringdon, over the former Midland main line to Bedford. South of the Thames, the units served Brighton from London termini and Bedford, shorter services using the

Below:
Reliveried in Thameslink colours, No 319379 leaves Blackfriars on a service from the Midland main line to Sutton on 11 September 1999. This unit is from the '319/1' batch, the second delivery, entering service in 1990.

Above:
Modified for use on Gatwick services, '4VEG' No 7911 (formerly '4VEP' No 7798) passes the original Gatwick Airport (Tinsley Green) platforms (1935-58) en route to Brighton via Redhill on 28 August 1979.

Class 458 returned to operation on Reading diagrams. Class 444s replaced Bournemouth's Class 442s, with Portsmouth services suffering the consequent imposition of inappropriate Class 450s on many main-line express diagrams, a level of service for which the class was not designed.

PARALLEL OPERATIONS 1
GATWICK

Services to Gatwick Airport became specialised when, in 1978, 12 '4VEP' units (Nos 7788-99) were altered internally to provide more luggage space. Classified '4VEG' and renumbered 7901-12, the units bore the legend 'Rapid City Link Gatwick-London'. Inevitably they were frequently to be found elsewhere on the system, given the vicissitudes of operation. A few years later, it was decided to upgrade the service, when Mk 2 locomotive-hauled vehicles were

return loop via Elephant & Castle, Sutton and Wimbledon. At first, Guildford (via Sutton) and Sevenoaks were served, but this was soon discontinued; it had not been reliable, with trains often turned back short of destinations – at Blackfriars and Sutton, for example. Initially operated by Network SouthEast, these units were divided between Thameslink and Connex South Central (later Govia Southern) at privatisation.

PARALLEL OPERATIONS 3
EUROSTAR

Class 373 units, already mentioned, comprised three batches, identified by allocation – Nos 373001-022 (North Pole, later Stratford, London), Nos 373101-108 (Forest, Bruxelles) and Nos 373201-232 (Le Landy, Paris).

SIGNALLING

The Southern Railway had been in the vanguard of the development of colour-light signalling, a detailed subject in itself and wholly outside the brief of this book. Suffice to say, the Southern installed the very first four-aspect colour-lights – anywhere in the world – inaugurated on 21 March 1926, between Holborn Viaduct and Elephant & Castle. Eighty years later, pockets of semaphore signalling survive and can still take the unprepared photographer pleasantly by surprise, as a most endearing anachronism.

LOCOMOTIVES

Three Southern Electric Raworth/Bulleid Co-Co locomotives were built, two in 1941 (later Nos 20001/2) and a third in 1948 (No 20003). They found employment on Newhaven boat trains, special services and freight, until withdrawal in 1968 (20003) and 1969 (20001/2). For the Kent electrification, 24 locomotives (Nos E5001-24) were constructed at Doncaster in 1959 and 1960. Used mainly for freight, they are remembered for their duties working the 'Golden Arrow'. They became Class 71 under the TOPS classification. 10 were later rebuilt as Class 74 electro-diesels (E6101-10), for use on the South Western Division when the Bournemouth route was electrified. Early withdrawal overtook both the '71s' and the '74s', given the preference for Classes 73 and 33.

Certainly Class 73 electro-diesels acquired, over the years, a distinctive Southern status. The first six (Nos E6001-06) were built in 1962, to be followed in 1967/68 by the delivery of a further 43 (Nos E6007-49). Their duties have covered every aspect of railway operation over the tracks of the former Southern Railway. They might, perhaps, now be principally remembered for their association with Gatwick Express. The first six were early casualties in Southern service, with all except two being dispatched to join the exiled Class 508 units on the Merseyrail third-rail system,

there to serve as works locomotives. They returned south, after a short time, as a focus for preservation. While many from the production series (formerly E6007-49) have been withdrawn, a significant few survive, in various liveries, attracting attention wherever they are to be found.

The Channel Tunnel link has since brought Class 92 freight locomotives over former Southern Railway metals, on services between Dollands Moor and Wembley, the staging post for points further north.

DEPARTMENTAL OPERATIONS

Traditionally, selected withdrawn units were adapted for 'internal use', examples from the very earliest pre-grouping stock through to second generation redundancies having been converted. Stores transporters, de-icing units, training units, leaf-clearing units etc all extended the lives of classes otherwise obsolete. New, purpose-built equipment is now the preferred choice of Network Rail, the successor to Railtrack.

CHANNEL TUNNEL RAIL LINK

With the opening of the 25kV high-speed link between St Pancras and Kent, the future is encouraging.

Below:
Eurostar sets Nos 373210/209 streak through Headcorn en route to the Channel Tunnel, on 3 September 2003.

Above:
Former three-car suburban unit No 1782, converted to a mobile instruction unit, stands at Fratton in April 1969. Here it carries the number S10 but this was altered to 053 when the unit was repainted in Rail blue.

Below:
Disbanded parts of '4SUB' No 4308 (originally three-car, new in 1925), can be seen on adjacent roads in Micheldever yard, October 1963. No S8144S donated parts to S8143S, for the latter's preservation in the National Railway Museum at York.

Right:
Motor coaches from unit No 4338 (originally built for the 1925 Eastern Section electrification) lie stored in Micheldever yard in October 1963 awaiting conversion to de-icing unit stock.

Below:
In November 1964, a down Brighton semi-fast, running via the 'Quarry Line', approaches Patcham Tunnel, formed of two '4-LAV' units.

Bottom:
In October 1966, '6CIT' unit No 3043 rounds the curve at Clapham Junction on a down Brighton fast service from Victoria in October 1966. The three '6CIT' units, Nos 3041-3, provided a larger proportion of first-class accommodation.

Above:
Class 5BEL unit No 3052 passes Clapham Junction B signalbox on the approach to Platform 13, *en route* non-stop to Brighton, in October 1966. In the background is Standard '82xxx' 2-6-2T on pilot duty from Waterloo.

Left:
'5BEL' No 3051, unsympathetically reliveried to suit BR's then corporate identity of Rail blue and grey, stands at Platform 13 at Victoria on 8 April 1972, awaiting departure for Brighton, beneath Eccleston Bridge.

Left:
A pair of '2BIL' units depart Fratton in October 1970 for Portsmouth Harbour on a semi-fast service from Brighton. No 2029 carries the (apparently) unvarnished version of BR(SR) green, a livery that quickly became tired and grubby. In the station, a '2HAL' waits on an up service, while a fairly new '4VEP' stands alongside the washing plant. In the distance, a '4COR' is parked in a non-electrified siding.

Right:
The unique '2BIL' No 2116 stands at the buffers to Platform 1 at Littlehampton in August 1968. As the last delivery of the third batch of '2BIL' units in 1937, No 2116 was the only example fitted with individual guttering over each door.

Below:
Worthing Central station opened in 1845 but the present buildings date from rebuilding in 1909. Here in August 1969, Rail blue-liveried '2BIL' No 2099 heads a train to Brighton that had originated in Littlehampton.

Right:
Horsted Keynes in July 1963, with '2-HAL' No 2630 (and a '2BIL') forming the service to Haywards Heath. With Headcode 37, the service originally operated between Horsted Keynes and Seaford.

Left;
Departing from Lancing in August 1969 is '2HAL' No 2603, coupled to a Rail blue-liveried '2BIL', on a stopping service from Portsmouth. The station has since been rebuilt but in this view the original 1845 buildings were still standing.

Left:
The cutting on the approach to Surbiton is host to '2HAL' No 2656, leading a six-car service to Alton in June 1969. Originally fitted with whistles, ex-Southern Railway units were latterly equipped with horns. The unit displays a full yellow end – but the absence of a black 'V' indicates this to be the vehicle without a guard's van.

Below:
In September 1969, '2HAL' No 2641 takes a stopping train from Brighton to Portsmouth away from Emsworth. The former goods yard had, by this time, been turned over to different commercial activity – seen to the right. The 'V' indicates the leading vehicle contains a guard's van area.

Right:
'4COR' No 3152 heads a 12-coach fast
service to Waterloo on 3 October 1965,
waiting to leave Platform 4 at Portsmouth
Harbour. The lever at the base of the door
droplight could fix the glass at any desired
height. The station at the Harbour had been
rebuilt for the electrification scheme of 1937.

Below:
In July 1968, '4COR' No 3121 heads a 12-car
rake on the climb to Witley from Milford.
The intermediate livery, here seen,
combined Rail blue with a small yellow
warning rectangle and white numerals.

Above:
Platform 9 at Brighton station on 8 April 1972, with '4COR' No 3140 in its last few weeks of operation, on an eastbound coastal service. No 3140 was part of the second batch of '4COR' units, delivered in 1937/38 for use on services to Bognor and Portsmouth, when the 'mid-Sussex' line was electrified. The unit here wears its final livery, Rail blue with full yellow ends.

Below:
The second Bulleid '4SUB' was delivered new in 1944. Here it is, unit No 4102, arriving at Raynes Park in June 1967, on a down Effingham Junction service, routed via Epsom.

Right:
A Woking stopping service leaves Walton on Thames, with original '4SUB' No 4108 leading, in June 1971. This unit, here re-liveried in Rail blue, had only a year to go before withdrawal in May 1972. Land occupied by the former goods yard is evident on the right of the picture, while the signalbox that stood at the south end of the island platform is here but a memory. There has been a station at this point since 1838, when the line was constructed.

Above:
In the 1970s, Epsom Downs terminus still had its spacious platform area, which was provided to cope with crowds attending Epsom race meetings. Here, on 15 June 1974, '4SUB' No 4384 of 1948 waits to return to Victoria. The line to Epsom Downs has since been reduced to the status of a long siding from Sutton. The original station area has been redeveloped, with a single platform – closer to Sutton – providing rudimentary passenger accommodation.

Right:
Victoria's Platforms 11 and 10 are seen in June 1974, prior to construction of the raft that, in 1983, replaced the ironwork and glazing, dating from the station's rebuilding in 1908. '4SUB' No 4636, awaiting departure for West Croydon, stands at Platform 11, while '2EPB' No 5753 brings up the rear of an arrival at Platform 10.

Left:
On 14 June 1983, '4SUB' No 4721 stands in Platform 4 at Sutton, which is the down line for Epsom Downs, service 92. No 4721 was one of several '4SUBs' to be roller-blind fitted. The railway reached Sutton in 1847 from West Croydon and was extended to Epsom Downs in 1868, when the 'Portsmouth Line' from Peckham Rye was opened. The 'Wall of Death' route to Wimbledon came 62 years later, in 1930.

Left:
Ten months after withdrawal, '4DD' double-deck unit No 4902 is seen at the South Eastern Steam Centre at Ashford in August 1972, having been saved for preservation. The unit was originally numbered 4002. The Centre was also the home of preserved '4COR' No 3142 for a period in the 1970s. [The French 4-6-0 seen here is no longer in this country.]

Below:
Herne Hill is the junction for Victoria and the line to Blackfriars, guarded by a signalbox, dating from the BR(SR) era. Here, on 14 August 1979, '4EPB' No 5174, together with another, heads for Orpington on a stopping service from Victoria. The unit still carries the all-blue livery. Herne Hill was opened in 1862 with the line to Elephant & Castle.

Above:
On 16 May 1982, Bulleid-profile '4EPB' No 5048, outshopped in blue/grey livery, calls at Peckham Rye on service 82, Victoria to Sevenoaks via Catford and Swanley.

Below:
Refurbished '4EPB' No 5421, on service 94 from West Croydon on 16 May 1982, approaches Battersea Park on the viaduct that has carried Brighton services into Victoria since 1860. The line here crosses the ex-LSWR main line into Waterloo.

Left:
Hurrying down from Polhill Tunnel in July 1980 is BR Standard '4EPB' Phase II No 5362, here still wearing the all-blue livery. A blue/grey '2EPB' is attached at the rear. Service 16 runs from Charing Cross to Sevenoaks.

Below:
A down service to Caterham is seen at Sydenham on 14 June 1983, formed of BR '4EPB' Phase I No 5328, with a '2EPB', still in the all-blue livery, bringing up the rear. Now extended, the original platforms were staggered.

Left:
Penge West, with '2EPB' No 5669 at the head of an eight-car train (four two-car units) to Caterham on 14 June 1983. The line was part of the original London & Croydon Railway, used by the SER for its services to Kent, via Redhill until the Sevenoaks 'cut-off' opened in 1868. Flimsy late-20th-century shelters on the down platform contrast strikingly with 19th century buildings on the up. The station opened in 1839.

Above:
Wimbledon island platforms Nos 9 & 10 are seen on 12 July 1985, with refurbished '2EPB' No 6324 working service 1, the West Croydon shuttle, since superseded by the Croydon Tramlink system. A then-new Class 455 No 5872 arrives at Platform 8 on a Guildford 'New Line' train, a service hitherto operated by '4VEP' units for a few years.

Below:
A four-car train, comprising two BR pattern '2EPB' units, enters Platform 4 at Clapham Junction on 14 May 1983. Unit No 5771 leads a Kingston circular service towards Waterloo.

Left:
The approach to Haslemere marks the summit of the long climb from Milford. Here in July 1968, Bulleid-profile '2HAP' No 5610 arrives on a stopping service to Portsmouth & Southsea. The unit has a 1950s body carried on frames dating from the 1930s, from '2NOL' units. The livery is intermediate, i.e. Rail blue with small yellow warning panel and white numerals.

Below:
Ewell West, on the line from Raynes Park to Epsom, opened in 1859. Original brick buildings survive. '4EPB' No 5781, together with two other '2EPB' units, arrives on a Dorking service from Waterloo on 18 May 1979. No 5781 was the first-numbered of 15 units transferred from the North East, when the Newcastle-South Shields line was de-electrified in 1963. These units were distinguishable from standard BR(SR) deliveries by their extended guard's van sections and smaller route indicator boxes.

Right:
Between Liss and Liphook, '2HAP' No 6101, in BR(SR) green livery, leads another of its class (in Rail blue) on a stopping service from Portsmouth & Southsea to Waterloo in July 1968. The '7' service indicator should here be '73'.

Right:
'2HAP' No 6070 leaves Sittingbourne on 17 August 1979, forming a semi-fast service from Victoria to Ramsgate, having come via Catford. The Sheerness on Sea branch service occupies the other side of the island platform. The line from Sittingbourne to Chatham opened for service in 1858 but electrification did not arrive until 1959, though it had reached Gillingham 20 years earlier, just prior to World War 2.

Below:
Between the tunnels at Guildford – Chalk and St Catherine's, north to south – '2HAP' No 6100 heads a 10-car peak-period fast service to Portsmouth on 21 April 1984, during a brief period of 10-car operation.

Above:
Aldershot station stands on the original line from Guildford to Alton via Tongham, opened throughout by 1852. However, the station at Aldershot was not opened until 1870, as a consequence of military expansion in the area and the contemporaneous development of the town itself. The station building is original, while the awnings feature both shallow pitched and circular arc styles. In this view from 24 August 1988, one of the then few '2HAP' survivors heads a 10-car train – the other two units are '4VEP' stock – on a Farnham service. The '2HAP' unit carries its final numerical identity, 4306.

Below:
The throat of the terminus station at London Bridge receives Bulleid-profile '2SAP' No 5631 (a declassified '2HAP') on 6 June 1981, operating a circular service from London Bridge, via St Helier and Tooting.

Windsor & Eton Riverside, the terminus of the branch from Staines, opened to traffic in 1849, shortly after the GWR had opened its branch from Slough. Here, in September 1974, '2SAP' units Nos 5939 and 5907 (until 1973 '2HAPs' Nos 6041 and 6007 respectively) stand either side of the north side platform, the outer face of which is no longer in use. The line from Whitton and Hounslow junctions to Windsor was electrified in 1930.

Below:
The eastern approach to Chichester station abuts the 1950s Southdown bus garage. Here '4CAP' No 3208 arrives on 12 April 1984 with a Brighton-Portsmouth stopping service. Roof clutter betrays the fact that the unit is formed from the first batch of BR-design '2HAPs'.

Left:
Fratton station, opened in 1885, is visited on 5 May 1984 by '4CAP' No 3303 on a stopping service to Brighton. '4CAPs' comprised pairs of '2HAP's in semi-permanent coupling; the 33xx-series units were from later 'HAP' builds.

Left:
Having emerged from Sevenoaks Tunnel (1mile 1,693yd), '4CEP' No 7192 heads an eight-car Margate (via Dover) service towards the descent through Hildenborough to Tonbridge on 5 August 1981.

Below:
Canterbury West goods yard, since redeveloped with housing, here hosts a newly-outshopped refurbished '4CEP' unit, No 411506, on public display, 4 May 1980. These units were refurbished at Swindon.

Above:
Martin Mill is on the joint SER/LCDR line from Buckland Junction to Deal, dating from 1881. '4CEP' No 1500, seen here on 29 May 1986, was unique, being the first to receive experimental internal refurbishment, after which it continued to carry its original identity, No 7153, for some time. Externally it was readily distinguishable from all later refurbishments as it retained its original (superior) sliding ventilators.

Right:
'4CEP' No 1553, in NSE livery, passes Orpington in September 1996 on service 18, Charing Cross to Margate, via Dover. The original station here opened in 1868, when the Sevenoaks 'cut-off' diverted traffic from the Redhill route.

Right:
In the vicinity of Birchington on Sea, a pair of 'Jaffa Cake'-liveried '4CEP' units race along on 30 May 1986, led by No 1588, on a fast service from Ramsgate to Victoria via Herne Hill. A public right of way is marked by a typical Southern Railway concrete footbridge at MP71.

Above:
An eight-coach 'CEP' formation in SWT livery completes the tortuous descent from Buriton Tunnel on a semi-fast service from Waterloo to Portsmouth Harbour on 2 May 1999. Unit No 1538 here takes the lead.

Left:
'4CEP' No 1592 was reliveried in traditional BR(SR) green for its last few months in service. On 3 September 2003 it enters Headcorn on a service from Ashford to Charing Cross.

Left:
Maidstone East opened in 1874, becoming part of the LCDR in 1879, with the route through to Ashford following in 1884. The station comprises two through platforms, a down side bay and a through centre road, reversible from the crossover east of Wheeler Street Tunnel. '3CEP' No 1108 is seen leaving on a service from Ashford to Victoria on 16 September 2002. No 1108 was one of a batch of 18 '4CEP' units to be reduced to three-car formation, instantly providing a higher power-to-weight ratio. No 1108 had started life, over four decades earlier, as '4BEP' No 7007.

Above:
'3CEP' No 1198 leaves Brockenhurst on a Lymington Pier shuttle on 5 September 2004. Subsequent to this unit's use, two '4CIG' units were reduced to three-car form for use on the branch. The line was opened in stages during the late 1850s. Ownership by the railway of the ferry service to Yarmouth (Isle of Wight) followed, when the station at Lymington Town was rebuilt.

Below:
'4BEP' No 7011, with a '4CIG' in tow, descends from the 1876 High Level at Portsmouth & Southsea on 10 August 1981 with a service to Victoria via Horsham. The Low Level part of the station was reduced to two platforms in the 1980s.

Above:
Coupled to a '4CIG' in the then new NSE livery, refurbished '4BEP' No 2306 enters Guildford on a fast service to Portsmouth Harbour on 4 September 1986. The substantial sub-station here dates from the 1925 Guildford via Cobham electrification.

Below:
The south end of Petersfield station sees the start of the climb to Buriton Tunnel. In this view, '4CEP' (formerly '4BEP') No 2317 addresses the task, forming a stopping service to Portsmouth & Southsea on 15 May 2003.

Right:
In the final months of service, the greyhound '4BEP' units exchanged their buffet cars for non-buffet coaches, taken from '4CEP' units. The '4BEP' units were then renumbered from 230x to 231x, while the donating '4CEP' units were renumbered in the 232x series, though their acquired buffet cars were effectively disbanded. On 18 October 2003, the last renumbered '4CEP', No 2327, here stands at Fratton.

Below:
On 17 April 1984 Motor Luggage Van No 68006 heads a boat train from Dover to Victoria, via Herne Hill, through Folkestone Warren. These single units later became Class 419.

Above:
Motor Luggage Van No 68010 is caught on 29 May 1985 passing Snowdown, leading a rake of '4VEP' units on service 30, Dover Priory to Victoria via Herne Hill.

Below:
Plenty of interest in the scene at Angmering, with semaphores, signalbox, station building and canopy all in view, in August 1969. The station dates from the 1846 opening of the line. Phase I '4CIG' No 7333 is seen on a service from Littlehampton to Victoria. This unit suffered early withdrawal, following a serious crash on the Brighton main line a few years later.

Right:
On 4 May 1980, Phase II '4CIG' No 7375 leads a 12-car 'CIG'/'BIG'/'CIG' formation through Platform 12 at Clapham Junction on a fast train from Hastings and Eastbourne, service 50.

Right:
Phase I '4CIG' No 1717, in NSE livery, passes Fishbourne signalbox on 12 April 1988, forming a Portsmouth–Victoria service. The closed road crossing here was formerly the main A27. The Lavant branch left the main line at the signalbox, where it took a northbound course which in earlier times carried trains through to Midhurst.

Below:
Renumbered Phase II '4CIG' No 1253 passes moribund Wimbledon yard on a stopping train to Woking, service 10, on 19 July 1988. The unit numbers are here in the traditional position, rather than beneath the grab rails.

Above:
Phase II '4CIG' No 1882, here renumbered for the second time and in NSE livery, approaches the climb to Buriton Tunnel on a semi-fast service from Portsmouth Harbour to Waterloo on 2 May 1999.

Below:
Greyhound '4CIG' No 1315, in SWT livery, arrives at Havant Junction in November 1997 on a fast service from Waterloo to Portsmouth & Southsea only (code 71). The Class 158, on a Brighton–Cardiff diagram, is waiting at the signal between Warblington and the junction. No 1315, as the first unit to be adapted, received twin headlights, a feature it retained when, along with all other units, it was fitted with a central light.

Above:
Phase I '4CIG' No 1731, in the colours of Connex South Central, departs from Cosham on 19 March 2001 as a Bournemouth–Victoria train, a service later to reverse at Southampton. The station here, opened in 1848, was a joint LBSCR/LSWR venture, pre-dating the direct route from Guildford to Havant by 11 years. Electrification of the route to Eastleigh and St Denys was completed in 1990.

Below:
On 19 September 2003, Phase II '4CIG' No 1851 approaches Hastings from Ore, *en route* to Victoria, via Eastbourne. It is one of a few such units that failed to receive the Connex livery, surviving in 'white', which was, perhaps, an act of conspicuous indifference to public image. The sidings seen beyond the EMU are those provided to serve the needs of diesel units on the non-electrified line from Ore to Ashford.

Above:
Emerging from the tunnel at Southampton on 30 October 2004 is Phase II '4-CIG' No 1854, recently outshopped in Southern livery. This service from the Brighton section would have terminated and reversed here. Southampton Central developed from the original station on the site, Southampton West (Blechynden), and was enlarged in the 1930s. The present up side buildings date from electrification.

Below:
The High Level at Portsmouth & Southsea, with a former '3COP', here restored to four-car formation, arriving on a service to Victoria, on 5 September 2004.

Right:
Phase I '4BIG' No 7032 leads a 12-car rake out of Quarry Tunnel, on a Brighton fast service, 28 August 1979. This route, known as the 'Quarry Line', opened in 1899 and released the LBSCR from the pressure of sharing a route with the SER.

Below:
'4VEP' No 7807 and another of its class form an Alton service, here seen at Walton on Thames. Both units wear the all-over Rail blue livery which was, by this time, June 1971, disappearing quickly.

Above:
On 13 June 1986, '4VEP' No 7731, in standard BR blue/grey livery, enters Horsham on service 32, having come from Victoria via Three Bridges.

Below:
'4VEP' No 7756 is here parked on the washing plant track at Lovers Walk, Brighton on 5 April 1980. All '4VEP' units had their horizontal sliding ventilators sealed, very soon after being delivered. This is one of two units to have had its sealed sliding window units replaced by plain glass panels.

Above:

Wearing intermediate numerical identity, No 3004 is one of the original batch of twenty '4VEP' units, here seen entering Guildford on a stopping service from Portsmouth & Southsea to Waterloo on 14 April 1988. Built for the Bournemouth electrification of 1967, the unit is here liveried in NSE colours. The car park, now multi-storey, occupies the site of the former steam mpd (70C).

Below:

Liss station, with the original down side building replaced by a steel-framed glazed structure, is visited by '4VEP' No 3434 in July 1991 on a stopping service to Portsmouth & Southsea. The unit carries its identity in the short-lived style, with numbers placed inconveniently beneath the grab rails. Apart from a few sub classes, '4VEPs' ended their days numbered in the 34xx and 35xx series.

Above:
Having emerged from Dover Harbour Tunnel (684yd), '4VEP' No 3562 passes the site of the former Hawkesbury Street Junction and approaches the remains of Dover Harbour station on 25 June 1998.

Left:
A pair of recently outshopped '4VEP' units with the window bars required for this route, heads a down service for East Grinstead at Oxted on 19 April 2000. The original station here was opened in 1884, jointly operated by the SER and the LBSCR. Electrification from Sanderstead, through Oxted, to East Grinstead took effect somewhat later, in 1990.

Left:
'4VEP' No 3411, here in SWT livery, was one of the original 20 delivered for the Bournemouth electrification. It awaits departure from Brighton on a Basingstoke service on 8 November 2004, while Class 377 units look on.

Right:
'4VEP' No 3809, one of a small (Porterbrook-leased) batch of renumbered units, enters Portsmouth & Southsea on a service from Southampton Central on 31 August 2003.

Right:
'4VOP' No 3919 arrives at Paddock Wood on service 13 from Maidstone West on 16 September 2002. This was the last of a batch of 19 '4VEP' units, declassified originally for the Connex 'South London Metro'.

Below.
'4REP' No 3010 passes Surbiton's Southern Railway signalbox in June 1969 on an up Bournemouth fast service. The rear four vehicles of this 12-coach train will have come from Weymouth, propelled to Bournemouth by a push-pull fitted Class 33/1 locomotive. Bournemouth line units, new in 1967, were repainted in blue/grey livery quite soon after entering service.

Above:
On 27 August 1983, '4REP' No 3004 heads a standard formation of 'REP'/'TC'/'TC' on an up service from Weymouth and Bournemouth to Waterloo, seen here east of Fleet.

Below:
Passing Worting Junction on the descent from Battledown flyover is a 12-coach Bournemouth and Weymouth train, with renumbered '4REP' No 2001 in charge. Full four-track availability between Waterloo and Worting Junction had been realised in 1909. At the time of the picture, 7 September 1988, '4REP' units were rapidly succumbing to withdrawal, their motors refurbished for use in Class 442.

Above:
Temporary formations abounded while the '4REP' units were being withdrawn for equipment recovery, for incorporation in Class 442. Here, unit No 2904 heads north through Shawford on 21 May 1988.

Below:
A semi-fast service to Bournemouth, with '4TC' No 433 being pushed by a '4REP', travels between Swaythling station, seen in the background, and St Denys on 15 August 1986.

Left:
On 29 May 1987, 'TC' unit No 8032, renumbered from the original 4xx series, is propelled through Micheldever on a semi-fast service to Bournemouth from Waterloo.

Left:
TC unit No 8004 is seen passing Lyndhurst Road, being propelled to Bournemouth on a semi-fast service on 17 August 1988. It is here reliveried in NSE style, with numbers placed beneath the grab rails.

Below:
No 508020 enters Wimbledon Platform 8, claiming to be bound for Strawberry Hill depot on 11 December 1982. The Southern Railway signalbox is behind the unit, with the tracks to Tooting and London Bridge far right. The first LSWR electric service ran from Waterloo to Wimbledon, entering via the line from East Putney, track currently used by District Line trains from Putney Bridge and Earl's Court.

Above:
Maidstone West was opened in 1844, when it was reached by the line from Paddock Wood. Twelve years later, in 1856, the line from Strood completed the north-south link. The northern section was electrified in 1939 but it was not until 1961/62 that electrification of the line to Paddock Wood took place. A small batch of Class 508 units, originally allocated to the South Western Division as four-car units, returned south from the Mersey third-rail system in later years, as three-car units. These have mainly been used on the Medway Valley line. In this view, dated 16 September 2002, No 508203 is about to depart on a service to London Bridge via Paddock Wood and Redhill. Meanwhile, No 508209 has arrived at Platform 2 on the shuttle service from Strood.

Below:
Unit No 5853, one of the first batch of Class 455 to be delivered, is about to leave Surbiton on a 'New Line' service to Guildford on 5 July 1988. Displacing '4VEP' units, first class was abandoned on this service. Surbiton station was rebuilt between 1936 and 1939 and survives as an architectural reminder of the Southern Railway self-confidence in its bold use of concrete modernism.

Above:
A 'New Line' service approaches the junction to the north of Guildford on 4 September 1986, formed of Class 455 No 5723, one of the sub-class incorporating trailers removed from Class 508. Note the SR vans in the siding.

Left:
Effingham Junction carriage shed, with the station in the background, on 25 June 1986. Here Class 455 No 5914 (one of the third batch), passes *en route* to Guildford, having come from Waterloo via Cobham. The eight-car train of Class 455 units to the right has come from Waterloo via Epsom, shortly to return to the up platform when No 5914 and its train have cleared the section.

Above:
On 21 September 2003 NSE-liveried No 455840 leaves Purley on a Redhill service. From the far platforms, tracks lead to Purley (Chipstead Line Junction), for the Caterham and Tattenham Corner branches. Purley station opened as Godstone Road in 1841. The lines were the subject of disputes between the Brighton and South Eastern companies, the latter operating the Caterham branch from 1859 and, later, building the Tattenham Corner branch in stages between 1897 and 1901.

Below:
Feltham station, here recently rebuilt, sees Class 455 No 5734 depart on a service to Weybridge on 8 October 2000. The vast marshalling yard, together with the motive power depot (that superseded Strawberry Hill, as electrification advanced after World War 1) was situated to the right of the line, on the London side of the station.

Above:
Class 455, as rebuilt for use on Southern suburban services. No 455839, seen here on 21 April 2007, has had its gangway connections removed. It is, perhaps, regrettable that the resulting glass panel was not employed to display a route code.

Below:
Class 455, as reliveried in SWT suburban style. Unit No 5906, a member of the third and final batch of units, is seen leaving Clapham Junction en route to Shepperton, service 24, on 21 April 2007.

Above:
Class 456 comprises 22 two-car units dating from 1990/91. No 456021 is still wearing its original NSE livery 16 years later, as it departs Victoria on 16 May 2007, forming a service to Epsom Downs.

Below:
On 21 April 2007, refurbished No 456004, looking very smart in its new Southern attire, leaves Clapham Junction on a service to Epsom, with another class member in tow.

Above:
Eastleigh station, where the elm tree on the down platform continues to survive all changes. Class 442 No 2402 awaits departure on a semi-fast service on 3 January 1998. The livery here was unique to this unit, being a modification of the standard NSE colour scheme, with the band of orange indicating Stagecoach South West Trains operation.

Below:
A single Class 442, in SWT livery, leaves Haslemere in May 1998 on a Waterloo service from Portsmouth Harbour. Jumper cable covers are here in place but there were periods when cables were exposed.

Above:
One of the first batch of 'Networkers', No 465013, arrives at Rochester in October 1998, on a stopping service from Gillingham to Victoria.

Below:
At Slade Green is situated the major servicing depot for suburban units on the lines to Dartford, once the site of a steam locomotive depot. 'Networker' No 465166 arrives over the junction from the Bexleyheath line, with a service to Charing Cross on 10 January 1998.

Above:
Reliveried for Connex South East, No 465017 approaches St Mary Cray Junction, on the former LCDR main line from Swanley on 28 April 1999.

Left:
On 3 September 2003, recently ex-works 'Networker' No 465213, one of the Metro-Cammell batch, takes the fast line through Headcorn on an ECS (empty carriage stock) working, probably bound for Chart Leacon. Connex branding is carried.

Right:
No 465905 is one of a batch of 34 Metro-Cammell 4652xx units rebuilt to include first-class accommodation for use on longer-distance services, when displaced by Class 376 on suburban routes. The unit is here passing non-stop through Kent House, on a service to Victoria on 16 May 2007.

Below:
Two-car 'Networker' No 466019 arrives at Crayford on 18 July 1998 on a Loop Line service from Dartford. It is here in original NSE livery.

Left:
Two-car 'Networker' No 466042 stands at Strood on 25 February 2006, waiting to leave for Maidstone West. It is in South Eastern livery and has had modifications to buffer beam and grab rails, a necessary measure in response to the need to deter uninvited guests from 'train surfing'.

Middle:
At Chatham on 16 September 2002, 'Express Networker' No 365505 bursts throught the temporary gloom of shade, where the enclosed footbridge and elegant elevated station building combine to form a covered section. The railway first served Chatham in 1858, as part of a piecemeal development, simultaneously to the east and to the west, becoming, when completed, the LCDR main line. The unit is one of 16 'Express Networkers', introduced on Connex SouthEast services. The sub-class has since been reallocated for 25kV operation on services out of King's Cross.

Below:
Two Class 319 units approach East Croydon from the south on 12 July 1988. No 319019, on the left, is on the up slow, its neighbour on the up fast. The units are in original NSE colours, the paler blue seen here being superseded by a darker shade, while the angled cab-end banding was replaced by a less severe curved feature. The land to the right here was formerly the site of Croydon Central station, opened in 1864 by the Brighton company, temporarily closed between 1871 and 1886 and finally closed in 1890.

Above:
The doyen unit, No 319001, leaves St Albans on 8 April 2006 in 25kV mode, on a service from the Midland main line to the Wimbledon loop. The unit carries an unusual livery, white with blue doors, since superseded.

Below:
No 319007 enters Kensington Olympia on 30 June 2003, on a service from Watford Junction to the Brighton main line. It here displays the Connex SouthCentral livery.

Above:
On 23 May 2007, No 319012 in Southern livery arrives at Elephant & Castle, on a northbound service. The unit is operating a First Capital Connect – former Thameslink – diagram to the Midland main line.

Below:
No 319361, in modified Thameslink livery, adapted for FCC as a temporary measure, rounds the curve from Loughborough Junction into Herne Hill on a southbound service on 23 May 2007.

Above:
No 319444 leaves Three Bridges *en route* to Brighton from the Midland main line, 23 May 2007. The unit carries the short-lived First Capital Connect livery, since superseded by First's national 'Urban Line' branding.

Below:
No 319427, recently outshopped in FCC 'Urban Line' livery, approaches Preston Park on the afternoon of 11 August 2007, with a train to Bedford.

Left:
A Eurostar formation arrives at Petts Wood Junction on 28 April 1999, having just traversed the down fast Tonbridge Loop from Bickley Junction. The South Eastern main line from Charing Cross is to the right.

Below:
On 14 August 2001, a Gatwick Express Class 460 unit glides smoothly through Clapham Junction, Platform 12, on a service from Gatwick Airport.

Left:
Class 458 unit No 8009 stands in the bay by the platform at Weybridge, forming a service to Waterloo via Staines, on 21 August 2002. The new station at road level contrasts with the original structures to the right, the footbridge and the platform awnings. Weybridge became a junction in 1848 when the line to Chertsey was opened, the line being extended to Virginia Water in 1866. Electrification followed in 1937.

Right:

Right:
Ramsgate depot during a period of major change, when 'Electrostars' were entering service, superseding the 40-year-old '4CEP' units and their younger partners, the '4VEPs'. Here, on 13 June 2001, No 375610 is operating a test run along the line to Ashford. It has yet to receive any declaration of ownership, travelling anonymously in unadorned white.

Right:
'Electrostar' No 375620 arrives at Chatham on a Ramsgate service, having just emerged from Fort Pitt Tunnel (428yd) on 16 September 2002. Rochester, on the other side of the tunnel, is only 44 chains distant. The unit here carries Connex SouthEast branding.

Below:
Canterbury West's famous elevated signalbox, at the Ramsgate end of the station, here sets the scene for the arrival on 29 June 2005 of 'Electrostar' No 375618 in South Eastern livery, on a Victoria via Maidstone East service.

Above:
One of the small batch of three-car units, No 375310, here leads a seven-car train to the Kent coast on 23 May 2007, having just emerged from the 1mile 381yd-long Penge Tunnel to pass Penge East station.

Left:
'Electrostar' No 375701 departs Ashford, Platform 6, on 16 May 2007 with a Canterbury West line service, with the Channel Tunnel express route forming a backdrop.

Left:
'Electrostar' No 375809 passes Penge East on an up service to Victoria on 23 May 2007. The station here retains original buildings; it was opened by the LCDR in 1863.

Right:
One of the 'Electrostars' with high-density 3+2 seating, No 375909 leads an up service from Ramsgate through Shortlands *en route* to Victoria on 23 May 2007.

Below:
Two almost brand new Class 376 inner suburban 5-car 'Electrostars' enter London Bridge on 27 April 2005, bound for Cannon Street, with No 376017 nearer the camera.

Left:
On 15 March 2006, 'Electrostar' No 377127 brings an East Grinstead service into Hurst Green, the line having been electrified from Sanderstead in 1990. The station here dates from 1907, 23 years later than the line itself. Concrete fencing, so typical of Southern Railway practice, provides platform screening. In the opposite direction, not here seen, a concrete footbridge spans the track just before the junction.

Below:
With rain cascading down on 22 September 2006, 'Electrostar' No 377210, in 25kV mode, waits at Watford Junction's Platform 10, forming a return service to the Brighton main line, via Kensington Olympia.

Left:
On 21 April 2007, 'Electrostar' No 377205, here in third-rail mode, has just arrived at Clapham Junction, Platform 17, on a service from Watford Junction, en route to the Brighton main line.

Right:
'Electrostar' No 375313 takes the canal cutting between Fratton and Portsmouth & Southsea, with a stopping service from Brighton on 27 July 2003. With modified couplings, the unit was later renumbered No 377303.

Right:
'Electrostar' No 377305 (formerly No 375315), enters East Croydon on 23 May 2007, coupled to another class member, on a fast service to Brighton from Victoria.

Below:
'Electrostar' No 377436 enters Pulborough on a down service to Bognor and Portsmouth on 18 February 2006. Semaphores and a well-maintained Brighton signalbox survive to provide contrast at a station opened in 1859, as a temporary terminus on the mid-Sussex route to Portsmouth. The line was extended from this point to Arundel Junction in 1863.

Left:
'Desiro' No 450010 stands in Platform 1 at Portsmouth Harbour on 24 May 2004, awaiting departure on a Southampton Central service. Note the removal of tracks in Platform 2 here.

Below:
Brand new 'Desiro' Class 444 units, with No 444019 leading, race through Weybridge on 23 April 2004 with a Portsmouth fast service. The new station building at road level is seen above '4VEP' No 3563, which waits in the bay platform on a shuttle service to Staines.

Left:
Southern Railway electric locomotive No 20001 arrives at Portsmouth & Southsea Low Level on 6 January 1964, with the Brighton-Plymouth train, during the short period when the service reversed at Portsmouth. This dispensed with the separate Portsmouth portion, attached and detached at Fareham. The picture is of the inaugural run, which was subsequently taken west by Pacific No 34072 *257 Squadron*.

Above:
On 31 May 1965, No 20002 stands at Portsmouth Harbour's Platform 1 ready to take Her Majesty The Queen back to London, when she travelled in Pullman car *Aquila*.

Right:
A general view of Clapham yard in March 1977 that takes in not only lines of locomotive-hauled stock but also two members of Class 74, enlarged rebuilds as electro-diesels from the E5000 class series.

Right:
In May 1967, an electro-diesel, from the later batch, cruises up to Popham No 2 Tunnel at Micheldever, with an eight-coach mixture, containing a buffet car. About six weeks later, steam ended on the Southern.

Above:
A Class 73, thought to be No 73118, travels south from Hilsea, *en route* to Fratton with a short freight train on 27 August 1982. 1B is here the code for Brighton-Fratton.

Left:
On 13 March 1983, a Class 73 powers the Venice-Simplon Orient Express (VSOE) Pullman car train from Victoria to Folkestone Harbour, via Catford (code 57). It is seen passing Paddock Wood.

Left:
Nos 73142 and 73129 double-head through Cosham on 16 April 1983, working the Railway Correspondence & Travel Society VSOE Pullman special.

Right:
In BR 'large logo' blue livery, No 73105 heads a Gatwick Express service through Salfords on 16 August 1984.

Below:
An unidentified Class 73 in InterCity 'large logo' livery drifts through Eastleigh on a short freight on 29 May 1987.

Right:
Wearing InterCity 'Swallow' Gatwick Express livery, No 73202, seen on 28 July 2004, rescues disabled Gatwick Express unit No 460001, which is about to be towed back towards Stewarts Lane, wrong line.

Left:
Now-preserved No 73101 *The Royal Alex'* uniquely carried the Pullman livery from 1991. It is here found on VSOE duty, parked in a reception road at Fratton on 3 May 1998.

Left:
EWS-liveried No 73131 passes Cosham on 19 September 2002, topping and tailing with Class 47 No 47790 on a Serco train.

Below:
A Class 73 in InterCity 'Swallow' Gatwick Express livery approaches Gatwick from Horley on 19 April 1999, the stock by this time reliveried in blue and charcoal with a red band.

Above:
Eurostar-adapted No 73130 runs through Kensington Olympia, light engine, *en route* to North Pole Depot on 30 June 2003.

Right:
At Purley, Main Line-liveried No 73136 is about to visit the Tattenham Corner branch with the 'North Downsman' railtour on 21 September 2003, with No 37194 at the other end of the train. No 73136 had replaced 'West Country' Pacific No 34016 *Bodmin* at London Bridge, the latter having failed.

Right:
SWT-liveried No 73109 is about to depart Fratton on 11 September 2003, towing '4CIG' No 1309, a unit which was, at the time, subject to frequent episodes of malfunction.

Left:
DMLV No 9104 leads a Gatwick Express formation through South Croydon on 15 July 2004, a station opened by the LBSCR in 1865, on a joint route, at the time, with the SER.

Below:
On 6 May 2000, No 92004 *Jane Austen* climbs through Barming with a freight from Dollands Moor, bound for Wembley.

SOUTHERN REGION ELECTRICS

Above:
Victoria LCDR was opened in 1860. In this view dated 14 February 1981, of Platforms 3, 4 and 5, '4VEP' No 7778, '2HAP' No 6161 and '4EPB' No 5324 form services to Ramsgate, Maidstone East and Orpington, respectively.

Right:
Platforms 4, 5, 6 & 7 at Waterloo on 9 July 1967, with '4SUB' No 4280, '2HAL' No 2610 and '2BIL' No 2050 at rest, oblivious of events further to the left of the picture, where the last rites of Southern steam were in full swing.

Right:
The new development at Charing Cross terminus towers over relatively new 'Electrostar' No 375630 on a service to Ramsgate, as the rain descends, on 17 May 2003.

Left:
Emerging from Crystal Palace Tunnel (746yd), '4EPB' No 5018 of 1953 takes the right fork at the junction on 16 August 1979, forming service 94 bound for West Croydon.

Below:
Refurbished No 455841 at Crystal Palace on 21 January 2002, *en route* from London Bridge to Victoria via Sydenham. Restoration of the fabric of this imposing edifice had, at this time, recently been completed.

Left:
'4SUB' No 4738, heading for Beckenham Junction, is here working wrong line through Crystal Palace, in response to an emergency arrangement on 14 August 1979. In the background is the grand main station building of 1856, carrying forward a vibrant memory of the West End & Crystal Palace Railway, linking Sydenham and Wandsworth Common. The section to Norwood Junction followed in 1857.

Right:
Clapham Junction 'A' signalbox, straddling the tracks at the London end, in its last years. '4EPB' No 5125 rushes into Platform 5 on 14 May 1983 with an anti-clockwise Hounslow Loop train. Electrification of the Hounslow Loop dates from 1916.

Below:
Virginia Water provides an almost perfect Southern Railway image in August 1971, the signalbox, enamel signage and station livery reporting the fashions of an earlier age. '4COR' 3124 heads a service to Aldershot, via Ascot, during the last full year of 'COR' operation, other units living out their final months on services out of Brighton, east and west. The line from Hampton Court Junction via Chertsey to Staines was opened to electric services in 1937.

Right:
Epsom station here receives the doyen Class 508, No 508001 *en route* from Waterloo to Effingham Junction (route 16) on 8 June 1984. The 'gantry' signalbox survived for several years after decommissioning, eventually being dismantled in the early 1990s. Alternate working at Epsom is dictated by the trackwork. The outer and inner faces of the up island platform serve Waterloo and Victoria services, respectively. On the down island, the order is reversed, with Victoria services arriving at the outer face. Class 508 was transferred to Merseyside when Class 455 arrived on the Southern in 1984. Electrification from Raynes Park came in 1925, through to Dorking North and Effingham Junction, four years ahead of the scheme that brought the third rail to the line from Sutton.

Left:
Dorking station, seen here on 25 June 1986, though rebuilt, retained original features on the island platform. Refurbished '4EPB' No 5436 takes a service to Victoria past the Southern Railway signalbox. The track plan seen here has since been rationalised considerably.

Below:
'3CEP' No 1106, heading for Paddock Wood on 6 May 2000, has just arrived at the staggered platform at East Farleigh, where attractive wooden buildings and semaphore signalling provide a period setting.

Left:
On 3 June 2006, 'Electrostar' No 377155 passes the attractively maintained signalbox at Berwick, a reminder of BR(SR) days. The box, at time of writing, controls the busy road crossing at this point.

Above:
Bournemouth Central, a grand edifice that has now, happily, been restored, was opened in 1899, 11 years after the completion of the direct route from the east. Here on 24 April 2003 '4VEP' No 3509, in South West Trains livery, arrives on a stopping service from Waterloo.

Right:
Dover Marine (later Western Docks) station opened to military traffic in 1915 and to public use four years later. On 2 October 1972 a pair of '4COR' units (Nos 3102/43) made a farewell tour of the Southern Electric system just prior to their withdrawal. Here they are seen taking a breather in Platform 4.

Right:
The site of Dover Harbour station (1861-1927) is here marked by surviving buildings, but no platforms, as '4VEP' No 3424, in an eight-car rake, winds round the sharp curve from the sea front on 25 June 1998. The train is here travelling on the surviving side of a triangle, once defined by Archcliffe Junction (to the south) and Hawkesbury Street Junction (to the north). Marine station, later renamed as Western Docks, occupied a position beyond the large building seen to the far left, the former SER Lord Warden Hotel.

Above:
Shepherdswell, opened in 1861, was the access point for colliery traffic over the East Kent Light Railway from Tilmanstone. On 29 May 1985 '4CEP' No 1545 forms the front part of a Victoria-Dover service. The 19th-century station building and awning stand on the down side, with wooden shelter and signalbox completing the scene on the up. Southern Railway concrete lampposts and hexagonal shades are here about to be replaced, with modern lighting already in position. Colour-light and semaphore signals were both in use here at this time.

Below:
Hollingbourne station opened in 1884, when the line from Maidstone East was extended to Ashford. '4CEP' 1580 arrives at the head of an eight-car train bound for Victoria from Ashford on 28 May 1985.

Above:

The EMU depot at Fratton was constructed for the electrification scheme of 1937. The carriage washing plant seen here survived in regular use for over six decades. In the right foreground '4CIG' No 1218 is seen in August 1991 with its (intermediate series) identity beneath the grab rails. The washing plant occupies the site of the former East Southsea island platform. Note lines of new Class 456 units, awaiting modification.

Middle:

Phase II '4CIG' No 1846 rushes past the maintenance depot at St Leonards with a stopping service from Ore to Brighton on 31 May 2000. Vehicles from Hastings diesel units, secured for preservation, are visible behind the 'VEP'/'CIG' formation, parked in front of the carriage shed that was constructed to serve the dieselisation of services between Hastings and Charing Cross and Cannon Street in the late 1950s. Electric multiple-units were originally serviced at Ore, to the east of Hastings, where a depot was constructed to the north of the platforms. It has since been abandoned.

Right:

Chessington South epitomises the Southern Railway's ultimate expression of modernism, with gravity-defying concrete structures dominating the scene. The branch proceeded no further but it was intended to extend to Leatherhead when construction ceased in 1939. After World War 2 the ideas were not rekindled. In the picture, Class 455 No 5727 has recently arrived from Waterloo on 25 June 1985, somewhat optimistically displaying 'Epsom' on the screen. Some hope!

Left:
The Wimbledon flyover, constructed in 1935/36, takes the up slow over the fast lines to join the down slow. The lead from the EMU depot enters bottom right. Unit No 5854 heads a Kingston circular on 19 July 1988.

Left:
The country end of the 1935/36 flyover at Wimbledon. On 19 July 1988, Class 455 5871, forming a Shepperton service, is being overtaken by an eight-car rake of '4VEP' stock led by No 3002, Basingstoke-bound.

Below:
Taken from the north side of the platform that became the one for International services, the yard at Ashford on 19 June 1982 contains a snowplough, '4CEP' units Nos 7206 and 1534 and a Class 33. The new fast line for Eurostar services now occupies the site of this former stabling point. '4CEP' No 7206 had started its life on peak period services between Waterloo and Portsmouth Harbour.

Above.
Brighton on 8 April 1972. Class 73 No E6029 displays code C7 (Brighton-London Bridge) and is on a train of vans. '4VEP' No 7799 is the front unit on a semi-fast service to Victoria, via the 'Quarry Line'. Alongside, '4COR' No 3130 is coupled ahead of '5BEL' No 3051 on a non-stop service to Victoria, an interesting nine-car combination at a time when the 'Brighton Belle' faced imminent demise.

Below.
Class 2BIL No 2099 leads another of its class on a stopping train to Portsmouth Harbour from Platform 2 at Brighton, while '2HAL' No 2656 rests in Platform 1, eventually to depart, all stations, for West Worthing.

Above:
Racing each other into Petts Wood on 7 March 1982 are two Phase I Standard profile '4EPBs', No 5310 displaying the code for Ashford and No 5338, arriving on a stopping service to Orpington from Charing Cross.

Below:
Chasing up the rise to St Mary Cray from Swanley on 14 February 1981 are rakes of '2HAP' and '4VEP' units. No 6084's train is from Ashford, via Maidstone East, while No 7770's is bound for Charing Cross, a train that will take the up Chatham Loop from St Mary Cray Junction to Chislehurst Junction.

Above:
The High Level island platform at Portsmouth & Southsea on 24 May 2004: '4VEP' No 3470 is on a stopping service to Waterloo, while 'Electrostar' No 377159 has just arrived on a train from Victoria.

Below:
Restored '4VEP' No 3417 (originally 7717) waits at Woking on 14 August 2004, alongside recently-delivered 'Desiro' No 450045. The '4VEP' is on a semi-fast to Bournemouth, while the Class 450 is on a Basingstoke stopper.

Above:
Contrasting liveries at Southampton Central: Phase II '4CIG' No 1865 waits to leave on a Victoria service, while Class 442 No 2415 forms a Waterloo train, on 30 October 2004. The footbridge here retains its 1930s form, though modern windows have since replaced Crittall originals. The up side rebuilding is here well in evidence. The original station clock tower was a costly sacrifice to modernisation.

Below:
Platforms 14 & 15 at Waterloo on 14 August 2004, many years after platform renumbering, following the creation of new Platforms 12 & 13. These had replaced the roadway, between Platform 11 and the former Platform 12, the latter becoming Platform 14, where Class 455 No 5847 is here seen on a Kingston circular via Richmond.
In Platform 15, '4CEP' (ex-'BEP') No 2312 is about to depart on a service to Portsmouth Harbour via Eastleigh.

Above:
Fratton island platform finds an '8CEP' formation arriving at the outer face on 16 November 2002 with a fast service from Waterloo. Unit 1553 is passing a Virgin IC125 (power cars Nos 43100/084), parked in the first reception line, with SWT Class 170 No 170305 in attendance on the second. By this time, Virgin 'Voyagers' were already replacing IC125s on services between the North West and Portsmouth.

Below:
'4COR' No 3158 heads a down Portsmouth fast service through Wimbledon in June 1967, with a Rail blue-liveried unit in the centre of the 12-car train. The station had been completely rebuilt in 1929, the surviving platform from the old layout, with awning, to the left in this view, serving a siding for vans and, latterly, engineering department wagons.

Left:
Just a few months old, a Class 442 unit speeds on its way to Bournemouth on 19 July 1988, while the raft for commercial development takes shape over the tracks at the country end of Wimbledon station.

Below:
Between Portsmouth & Southsea and Fratton, the railway follows the line of the former canal. '4COR' No 3107 is here in charge of a 12-coach fast train to Waterloo in August 1962.

Left:
Almost brand new, 'Desiro' No 450057 and another of its class travel through the former canal cutting between Portsmouth & Southsea and Fratton with a service to Waterloo via Eastleigh on 15 June 2004.

Right:
'2HAL' No 2609 leaves Littlehampton in August 1968 *en route* to Brighton, the code here probably being incorrect. The goods yard has since become storage space for multiple-units. The station opened in 1863.

Below:
Phase II '4CIG' No 1845, heading to Bognor, passes Phase I '4CIG' No 1747 in the storage sidings at Littlehampton on 29 May 1999. Meanwhile, Class 5 4-6-0 No 73096 takes water in the background. The Phase II '4CIG' carries both a crude yellow patch on the roof and '1' numerals flanking the cab windows to guide first-class passengers to their desired accommodation.

Right:
While BR's last timetabled main line steam services were running their course 250 miles away, '4COR' No 3120 leads a 12-car rake through Lewes with an up Newhaven boat train on 4 August 1968. A fine display of semaphores then guarded the station exit; now displaced, they are survived by the elegant signalbox, still in use at the time of writing. The station here dates from 1889, since rationalised, in response to operating requirements.

Above:
'Electrostar' No 377443 arrives at Lewes on 30 January 2006, bound for Victoria, in crisp winter afternoon sunshine. The new footbridge is visible behind the surviving signalbox.

Below:
Eastleigh Carriage Works in July 1963, with former Tyneside units being rebuilt as '2EPB' units for use on Southern suburban services. These 15 units had larger guard's van space than the BR-pattern 'EPBs' which spent their entire career on the Southern.

Above:
'4SUB' No 4654 stands in Platform 1 at Waterloo on 6 March 1982, awaiting departure on a Dorking service. The original station opened on 11 July 1848. Rebuilding, begun by the LSWR, was completed by the Southern but the new 21-platform station was officially opened on 21 March 1922, just prior to the Grouping

Right:
Phase II '4CIG' No 1831 stands in Platform 3 at Brighton on 27 November 2004, about to leave on a stopping service to Portsmouth Harbour. Television monitors had, by this time, provided platform information for many years. Platform 3 at Brighton uniquely has access to all directions, west, north and east.

Right:
Stores unit No 024 arrives at Ashford on 11 August 1979 on one of the diagrams then operating, connecting Eastleigh, Selhurst and Ashford. These motor coaches were from '4SUB' unit No 4378. The platform from which the picture was taken was later requisitioned and rebuilt to serve the needs of Eurostar international traffic. A further island platform, to the north, was built as a replacement for local traffic.

Above:
Phase II '4CIG' No 7402 is caught arcing as it enters Barnham
Junction from Bognor Regis on 23 May 1982. The attractive station-
mounted signalbox stands on the left of the picture, with semaphores
and a sub-station almost framing the unit's arrival. The station,
known as Barnham Junction until 1929 and just Barnham thereafter,
opened to traffic in 1864.

Below:
'4CEP' No 411600 stands at Bromley South on 16 May 1982, heading
a Ramsgate service, one that has travelled via Catford (code 51).

Left:
The roof line of both '4CEP' design and that of the awnings at Bromley South are here illustrated, with unit No 7188 at the front of a service from Dover, via Canterbury East, on 16 May 1982. The station was modernised for the Phase I Kent Coast electrification of 1959, when the tracks were paired differently, fast and slow pairs superseding directional pairs. The original station here opened in 1858 as part of the Bromley Junction to Bickley section of new main line.

Below:
Phase I '4CIG' No 1751 charges through the shallow cutting between Clapham Junction and Wandsworth Common on 5 April 2003. This train would have divided at Haywards Heath, the leading unit proceeding to Southampton (code 46), with the rear '4CIG' following on to turn left at Keymer Junction for Eastbourne.

Bottom:
'4EPB' No 5011, of 1952, enters Sutton on 18 October 1975 with a service from London Bridge, travelling beneath the gantry bearing an array of semaphores. Platform 4, which it is using, takes trains on to Epsom Downs.

Above:
On 5 September 2004, Weymouth receives '4CEP' (ex-'4BEP') unit No 2311 (with 2313 in tow) on a valedictory tour by the class from Portsmouth Harbour.

Left:
The Ouse Valley Viaduct, with pavilions stationed at each of its four corners, is here host to Phase II '4CIG' No 7428, at the head of a service from Littlehampton to Victoria, code 16, in August 1975.

Left:
The mechanical Southern Railway departure board on the station concourse at Brighton, seen here on 1 April 1985, was as fascinating as it was practical – inventive, attractive and effective, very much a fitting tribute to all that is conjured up by those two magical words – Southern Electric!